PERSONALITY
Plus
FOR COUPLES

Other books by Florence Littauer

Personality Plus for Parents

Personality Plus

Personality Puzzle with Marita Littauer

Put Power in Your Personality!

Getting Along with Almost Anybody with Marita Littauer

Talking So People Will Listen with Marita Littauer

Shades of Beauty with Marita Littauer

Why Do I Feel the Way I Do? with Fred Littauer

Daily Marriage Builders with Fred Littauer

After Every Wedding Comes a Marriage with Fred Littauer

Freeing Your Mind from Memories That Bind with Fred Littauer

Taking Charge of Your Life

How to Beat the Blahs

Blow Away the Black Clouds

It Takes So Little to Be above Average

How to Get Along with Difficult People

Out of the Cabbage Patch

I've Found My Keys, Now Where's My Car?

Silver Boxes

Dare to Dream

Raising Christians, Not Just Children

Your Personality Tree (also available as video album)

Hope for Hurting Women

Looking for God in All the Right Places

The Gift of Encouraging Words

Get a Life without the Strife with Fred Littauer

For information on having Florence speak to your church or group, call CLASSERVICES: 1-800-433-6633.

PERSONALITY *Plus* FOR COUPLES

Understanding Yourself and the One You Love

FLORENCE LITTAUER

Fleming H. Revell
A Division of Baker Book House Co
Grand Rapids, Michigan 49516

Published by Fleming H. Revell
a division of Baker Book House Company
P.O. Box 6287, Grand Rapids, MI 49516-6287

Printed in the United States of America

Library of Congress Cataloging-in-Publicaton Data

Littauer, Florence, 1928–
    Personality plus for couples : understanding yourself and the one you love / Florence Littauer.
      p.   cm.
    Includes bibliographical references.
    ISBN 0-8007-5764-5 (pbk.)
    1. Typology (Psychology) 2. Man-woman relationships. 3. Man-woman relationships—Religious aspects—Christianity. 4. Christian life. I. Title.
BF698.3 .L55 2001
155.2′6—dc21
                                         2001048226

For current information about all releases from Baker Book House, visit our web site: http://www.bakerbooks.com

A special thanks to Tammy Bennett and Rose Sweet
for their creative stimulation and words of encouragement.
FLORENCE LITTAUER

CONTENTS

5

INTRODUCTION

Once upon a Time . . .

Back in the good old days when I was young, all fiction had the same plot: The beautiful princess is the catch of the town, all men pursue her, some are villains, the handsome prince slays the undeserving, the princess leaps into his arms in gratitude, and they fall in love, get married, and . . .

When I run through this litany at conferences I can always count on the crowd to finish this fairy-tale plotline for me. We all know the prince and princess always go on to live "happily ever after," right?

But did you ever notice that those fairy tales all end with the wedding? They don't even review the honeymoon and surely don't touch on the trauma of discovering that this person is nothing like you and disagrees with your opinion on things as basic as buttering toast.

For Fred and me it was the grapes. We were sitting on the patio of a pink cottage in Bermuda when the waiter brought us a platter of fruit. I was excited with the service and began to talk to the grapes. (I frequently talk to inanimate objects when no one else seems to be listening.)

"What a cute little fellow you are," I said to a grape. "I think I'll eat you first."

As I was chatting sociably with the fruit, Fred turned towards me and asked, "Do you like grapes?"

I thought that was an unnecessary question since I was happily eating the grapes. But submissive bride that I was, I smiled and answered, "Yes, I like grapes."

"Then I assume you'd like to know how to eat them properly," he responded.

I had no idea there was a proper way to eat grapes, but being polite, I asked, "How do you eat grapes properly?" I had already learned that in Fred's family everything had to be done politely and properly.

"First you take out your nail clippers," Fred instructed.

I didn't have nail clippers, but Fred did. Fred has enough equipment in his pockets to outlast the cast of *Survivor*. He has a minimum of nine pens with him, even on vacation: red, blue, and black, with fine tip, medium tip, and felt tip. And not only does Fred have his pens, his nail clippers, his Swiss army knife, and his keys, but they are always in the same pocket so he can produce them quickly with no fumbling.

"Then you clip a small cluster of grapes from the larger bunch," Fred explained as he took out his nail clippers, selected a little cluster of grapes, and snipped them off at the main stem.

"Do they taste better that way?" I asked, confused by why this procedure was so important.

Fred looked at me with pity. "It has nothing to do with the taste. It's to preserve the shape of the bunch."

Now I didn't know who cared about how the bunch looked, so I turned around to see if there were any grape judges hidden in the bushes. Seeing none, I asked, "What difference does it make?" I had not yet learned one does not question Fred's statements without expecting to receive a simplistic lesson appropriate for a first grader.

"When you eat grapes the way you are doing," Fred said with an air of superiority, "you will notice that there are little ugly brown stems sticking up all over the bunch."

I looked. Sure enough, there were ugly brown stems sticking up. But they didn't bother me, so I still didn't understand the problem. I hadn't yet learned that my opinion didn't matter if the situation bothered him.

This grape-eating situation was just the first of many that revealed my new husband's penchant for attention to every detail.

When we'd been married only two weeks, we went to a movie one night. On the way home I had an idea. "Could we stop and get an ice cream cone?" I suggested.

Without hesitation, Fred said no.

Now I wasn't used to this. "What do you mean 'no'?" I asked.

"I mean, no you can't have an ice cream cone." Fred's answer was simple enough, but it didn't really answer my question, so he continued. "You will have to learn that every morning I make out my schedule for the day. From here on, if you wish to have ice cream at 11:00 at night, you tell me at 7:00 in the morning when I make out my schedule."

"But I didn't know at 7:00 this morning that I would want ice cream at 11:00 tonight," I protested. Unfortunately for me, my argument wasn't very persuasive for Fred. I didn't get my ice cream.

I often share these stories at conferences where I speak. And it's at about this point that Fred bursts through the audience, grabs the mike, and remarks, "I bet you think she's a lot of fun to live with!"

Some members of the audience are afraid he's mad at me, some laugh, and a few applaud as if to say, "Yes, she is fun to live with." (I always encourage that last group and get everyone clapping with me.) While all of this is happening, Fred looks disturbed and begins to tell tales about me.

"I want you ladies to know that after I married Florence there were many significant changes in my life." Fred states this with an air of perfection and disappointment. "Before I got married my toothpaste tube was always neat and tidy, but after we got married it turned ugly. I began to watch Florence to see what in the world she was doing with the toothpaste."

Fred watched me a lot. And he not only watched, but he felt led to tell me how not to make that mistake again.

"Of course, she's talking all the time and paying no attention to what she's doing," Fred continues with his description of my appalling toothpaste habits. "She picks up the toothpaste and squeezes it in the middle," he groans, seeking sympathy from his fellow neatniks in the crowd. "It pours out of the top and gets the whole tube all sticky. Then she takes her brush and smears it across the top. Sometimes she puts the cap on and sometimes she doesn't. It's a mess either way."

At this point the neatniks like Fred are feeling sick, and the ones like me are sympathetic and hoping Fred doesn't yell at me.

"But I've solved the problem," he says brightly as he looks toward the audience for the answer. "Two tubes" they call out, proud of their quick response.

"That's right," Fred says with a smile. "Two tubes. She has her own tube, and she can squeeze it whatever way she wants. But when it gets real messy she hands it to me and says, 'Here, Fred, will you straighten this out please?'"

Fred gives a satisfied smile. "So I lay it down on the counter and smooth it out. She gets another month out of it, and we've saved money."

As he smirks triumphantly, I jump in. "The reason I give him the toothpaste—"

Before I can finish he moves in front of me and comments, "People with Florence's kind of personality tend to interrupt a lot."

I counter with, "Those of you like me know that we don't really see it as interrupting. It's just that what we've got to say is more interesting than what the other person is saying." The women in the audience laugh in agreement.

After the laughter dies down a bit, I repeat my earlier statement. "The reason I give the tube to Fred is not because I care how it looks. I don't. But Fred goes through the trash. If he can find anything with any shred of redemptive value, he will take it out, wash it up, and show me how to use it again."

By this time everyone in the audience has related to one of us and has taken sides according to their own personality.

How about you? Are you the one who wants to have fun, be spontaneous, and ignore schedules? Or do you feel that without a tight schedule, life would be no fun?

Whatever your personality, you will find it in the real-life examples in this book. You women will find yourselves and see why your husband is so difficult to live with. You men will relate quickly to your strengths and wonder why you married the one woman in the world who doesn't see your virtues.

By the time you have finished reading, you will look at each other differently and realize what God had in mind when he brought you together to live "happily ever after."

PART 1

Setting the Stage

An Overview of the Personalities

one

A CAST OF CHARACTERS

What Are the Personalities?

We each come into this world with our own set of inherited traits. These traits are often a blend of our forebears, but they are not necessarily an exact copy of any one person. Sometimes the shy, quiet, and thoughtful mother is amazed to find that she has a loud, aggressive, argumentative child. My own mother often said of me, "You're just like Ruth!" (This was not meant to be a compliment, as her sister Ruth was known as a charming manipulator.)

It does not take most married couples very long to realize that they have different personality traits. Often these differences make marriage exciting as each spouse enjoys the unique personality of the other. Sometimes, however, these differences become downright perplexing, with neither spouse understanding how the other feels.

A friend of mine wrote to tell me of the trip she and her family took to the Holy Land. During their journey through Israel, Jordan, and Egypt, she had stones thrown at her, and she got both food and water poisoning. Her son Jon was hit with rubber bullets at one place, and was hit three times by rioting natives at another location.

When they returned home and began telling others about their trip, she was amazed at how different her and her husband's perspectives were. While she described being terrified the whole time, her husband was rejoicing in his opportunity to pray at so many holy sites around the Sea of Galilee and Bethlehem. She expressed relief at being out of the dangerous situation. He recommended that others visit the Middle East for a "safe" time because he felt the good experiences had exceeded his expectations!

So how can two people have such completely different views of the exact same experience?

It's All Greek to Me

It was over two thousand years ago, before Christ walked on this earth, that a Greek intellectual philosopher and physician first began to realize that all people are not alike. Hippocrates first noticed that in addition to having different looks, hair texture, eye color, and body shape, people also have unique personalities that set them apart. He attempted to explain these differences by categorizing people according to the chemicals in their bodies. Around 400 B.C., he identified four bodily fluids— blood, yellow bile, phlegm, and black bile—that he believed accounted for differences in personalities.

Centuries later, around A.D. 149, a Roman physiologist named Galen proposed a temperament theory that built on Hippocrates' observations. According to Galen, four basic human personalities—Sanguine, Choleric, Melancholy, and Phlegmatic—were possible, depending on the amount of certain bodily fluids that were in a person's body.

Of course, later scientists reexamined these ideas and discovered that the four bodily fluids do not really cause behavioral differences. But despite Hippocrates and Galen's failure to get it right, more recent developments have shown that there is more truth to their theories than was once supposed. Though our personalities are not believed to be caused by bodily fluids, current work in the field of genomics has shown that our personalities are linked to a different physical source: our genes.

New Discoveries

When I first began my study of personalities back in 1968, there was little tangible evidence to prove that our personality was included in our genes. Hippocrates said so. Karl Jung said so. Like them, I too believed we inherit our personality. But the theories didn't have current proof. During the '90s, new evidence was found when a geneticist reported that he could isolate inherited human traits, and that personalities were among the easiest to trace.

As new proof emerged I became more and more excited. I no longer needed to hope people would believe me. I could now prove to them that we do come into this world with a personality pattern. I could give them scientific evidence that we are, in a way, a prepackaged personality.

Cover articles on genomics suddenly appeared. On July 3, 2000, *Time* magazine's cover read, "Cracking the Code: The Historic Feat That Changes Medicine Forever," and a few months later their February 19, 2001 issue proclaimed, "Human Cloning Is Closer Than You Think." Major newsmagazines and newspapers featured stories and articles about the Human Genome Project and its efforts to map out the genetic material that makes up human beings. *USA Today* summed up these amazing developments when their February 12, 2001, Life section read "Decoding the Mysteries of Life: Human Genome Makes Mind-Boggling Reading."

Reading about this exciting subject is indeed mind-boggling! No man millions of years ago could have thought up the idea that thirty thousand genes make up a human being. And yet, our Greek friends weren't completely wrong when they suspected that human personalities are linked to our physical makeup. Though we now know that the personalities are not caused by varying levels of the four bodily fluids, we have confirmed that our personalities are caused by the physical combination of our genes.

The Amazing Creator

Even as we consider the wondrous discoveries that modern science has made, we must never forget the One who created these mysteries.

"It is not possible to step on God's toes," says Neale Donald Walsch in his book *Conversations with God.* Referring to his study of genomics, he explains, "I think God chuckles at our astonishment at these rather primitive revelations, very much as we smile at a child's first mastery of multiplication tables."[1]

God indeed may chuckle when we take that first look at our newborn. "He's got my blue eyes, your long fingers. . . ." We expect our children to be like us, but we seldom think of it in terms of genetics or God. Fortunately, we don't have to understand all the complexities of genetics. We have a genius God whose ways are beyond what our limited minds can understand. He can take genes from each parent, mix them together, and produce a one-of-a-kind creation.

God did not create us to be born with an empty mind, waiting for the obstetrician to fill it up at birth. Who knows what we'd be like if it were up to a human? If he had a bad day, he might make all troublemakers. Or on a great day, he might create a row of little angels.

Instead, the years of genetics research have validated the Hippocratic hypothesis that we do inherit our coloring, shape, abilities, and most important for our study together, our personalities. The amazing reality is that God created each person to have a unique combination of thousands of genes. With all the new proofs of our inherited traits, even atheists must wonder who put this all together!

18

1. *USA Today* (February 12, 2001)

Introducing the Famous Four

Although each individual is unique, there are personality traits that can be grouped in categories that make it easier to understand who we are and why everyone is not just like us. Our personalities can be broken into four basic types. I've chosen to give Greek terms to them: the Sanguine who is the Popular Personality, the Melancholy who is the Perfect Personality, the Choleric who is the Powerful Personality, and the Phlegmatic who is the Peaceful Personality.

The Popular Personality—Sanguine

The Sanguine types are the fun-loving, sunny, outgoing personalities who draw people to them because they seem to be having such a good time. They would be the ones to place a bumper sticker on their car reading, "Are we having fun yet?" Often they can't remember where they are headed, they lose their keys, and they're prone to talk too much. They can turn a trivial event into a soap opera that grows more dramatic with each storytelling. They are humorous and fascinating and never let the truth stand in the way of a good story. In their charming way, they will coyly tell you that they are not lying—they are just "remembering creatively."

Sanguines seek the attention, affection, approval, and acceptance of those around them. These boisterous individuals bring fun and drama into almost any situation, love the spotlight, and enjoy motivating others. They initiate conversations and can instantly become best friends with everyone in a group. Sanguines are usually optimistic and almost always charming. However, they can also be disorganized, emotional, and hypersensitive about what others think of them.

About a Sanguine person you might make comments such as, "She talks all the time" or "He never met a stranger." You may call this person the "talker."

The Perfect Personality—Melancholy

The opposite of the fun-loving Sanguines, and the one they usually marry, is the Melancholy: deep, thoughtful, introspective, serious, and perfectionistic. Their motto is: "If it's worth doing, it's worth doing right!" They have difficulty seeing that they have any faults because they innately do everything right and can always show that the current problem is someone else's fault. They feel led to correct their Sanguine mate's embellished statistics, slowing down an otherwise exciting story.

With perfection as their goal, they often go through life downcast, discouraged, and depressed over the sins of others—especially over the blatant faults of their mate. "What is the matter with you?" they ask.

Melancholies need sensitivity and support from others, and they require space and silence in which to think before they speak, write, or act. They are task-oriented folks who are careful and organized. These perfectionists thrive on order, and you can depend on them to complete a job on time. But their perfectionism may make them critical or pessimistic, and they drive themselves crazy with their efforts to measure up to their own high standards.

When speaking about the Melancholy, you'll likely say, "She is so together" or "He is such a perfectionist." You might call this person a "thinker."

The Powerful Personality—Choleric

As Melancholies *think* they're right, Cholerics *know* they are. Even if everyone in the room opposes their ideas, they will still forge ahead to get their way. Opposition only fortifies their determination. These people, male or female, young or old, are programmed to put more emphasis on getting their own way than on getting along with others or having people like them. There is little point in arguing with this person. You haven't got a chance. However, in a group, Cholerics become the presidents, get the work done, and don't waste time on foolish talk. They are the dynamic leaders of life and their motto echoes Nike's slogan of "Just do it!"

Cholerics seek loyalty and appreciation from others. They strive for control and expect credit for their achievements. They love being challenged and easily accept difficult assignments. Their self-discipline and ability to focus make them strong leaders. But their drive and determination can cause them to become workaholics, make them opinionated and stubborn, and leave them insensitive to others' feelings.

Of the Choleric you may say, "He really gets in your face" or "If you want to get something done, ask her." You would call this person the "doer."

The Peaceful Personality—**Phlegmatic**

Strong-willed Cholerics gravitate toward Phlegmatics who will agree with them and not cause them any trouble. It's not that the Phlegmatics aren't bright; actually, they are smarter than the rest of us. They know that a sweet, pleasant personality will cause others to do their work. They think in terms of conserving energy and feel that if you ignore something long enough, someone else will do it. They are easygoing and diplomatic, but don't move fast enough for most Cholerics. In marriage, the Cholerics are constantly nagging the Phlegmatics to work faster, but the Phlegmatics learn to tune them out, sticking to their own motto of "Don't sweat the small stuff."

Phlegmatics dislike risk, challenge, and surprise and will require time to adapt to changes. Although they avoid situations that are too stressful, they can work well under pressure. However, their lack of discipline and motivation often allows them to procrastinate in the absence of a strong leader.

Phlegmatics are reserved, but they enjoy being around people. Although they don't have the need to talk as much as the Sanguine, they have an innate wit and seem to say the right thing at just the right time. They are steady and stable, and because

21

they are security-oriented, they like to create safety for their spouses and children. They seek peace and quiet and tend to act as negotiators instead of fighters. These loyal individuals find worth and respect in providing for their families and assisting people who need help.

When referring to the Phlegmatic, you may say things like, "He is such a nice guy" or "She is so sweet." You would view this person as a "watcher."

The following chart summarizes the basic characteristics of each personality type.

Popular Sanguine	LEAD — Extroverted • Optimistic • Outspoken	Powerful Choleric

Basic Desire:
  have fun
Emotional Needs:
  attention
  affection
  approval
  acceptance
Controls by:
  charm
		Basic Desire:
		  have control
		Emotional Needs:
		  loyalty
		  sense of control
		  appreciation
		  credit for work
		Controls by:
		  threat of anger

PLAY Witty • Easygoing • Not goal-oriented		WORK Decisive • Organized • Goal-oriented
Peaceful Phlegmatic	ANALYZE — Introverted • Pessimistic • Soft-spoken	Perfect Melancholy

Basic Desire:
  have peace
Emotional Needs:
  peace and quiet
  feeling of worth
  lack of stress
  respect
Controls by:
  procrastination
		Basic Desire:
		  have perfection
		Emotional Needs:
		  sensitivity
		  support
		  space
		  silence
		Controls by:
		  threat of moods

Partnering Personalities

Every person is born with a predisposition toward one (or more) of these four personality types. Most of us are a combination of two personalities. Sometimes they are balanced evenly, but usually one is predominant.

There are four natural combinations of personalities that occur when any two adjoining squares are combined from the personality chart above. The top two cells—Sanguine and Choleric—combine naturally because both types are extroverted, optimistic, and outspoken. This combination results in a highly excitable and charming individual who is energized by people. Sanguine/Choleric spouses are the type who want to have fun and be in charge of the games.

The Melancholy and Phlegmatic cells at the bottom of the chart combine well because both personalities are introverted, pessimistic, and soft-spoken. The Melancholy/Phlegmatic spouse will like things to be perfect if it's not too much like work. A Melancholy/Phlegmatic will be less excitable and more drained by people. It's dealing with people that wears out these individuals. At their best, Melancholy/Phlegmatics do things perfectly and on time while being pleasant and nonconfrontational. At times, however, their nit-picking nature will leave them depressed and too drained to accomplish anything.

The personalities on the right side of the chart—Choleric and Melancholy—combine to produce a highly task-focused individual. The Choleric/Melancholy spouse wants to be in charge and make it all perfect. This combination will result in the greatest achiever, doing things quickly while wanting everything to be perfect. But they may become bossy and manipulative or get discouraged that no one does anything right or on time.

The Sanguine and Phlegmatic personalities on the left side of the chart also combine easily, resulting in a very relationship-oriented person. The Sanguine/Phlegmatic spouse likes to have fun if they don't have to go somewhere to do it. This combina-

23

tion makes everyone's favorite friend—Sanguine fun with an agreeable and easygoing Phlegmatic nature. They may tend, though, to be undisciplined or sarcastic and unwilling to *do* anything. They easily forget their responsibilities but can always charm someone else into doing them.

Can Opposites Be One?

Each of us was born with a particular personality or natural combination, but some individuals seem to display traits of apparently opposite personalities. You may see yourself as a Peaceful Phlegmatic at home but a Powerful Choleric as soon as you step into the office. Or perhaps you find yourself compulsively organizing things, as you'd expect from a Perfect Melancholy, but your favorite pastime is performing on center stage as the life of the party. How can that be? Do opposite personalities really combine?

When the two sides of an individual's personality have many traits in common, such as the Sanguine/Choleric and Melancholy/Phlegmatic, their combinations are usually quite balanced. In contrast, Choleric/Melancholy or Sanguine/Phlegmatic combinations join opposite traits like optimism and pessimism, excitability and unexcitability, and outgoing tendencies with reserved tendencies. Consequently, these individuals tend to be less balanced, leaving them with a personality that is predominantly one or the other.

While it's true that many people *function* in opposing personalities depending on the circumstances, most often such individuals don't really *possess* such a personality. In some cases, we actually attribute certain characteristics to the wrong personality type. Without completely understanding both the behavior and the motivation for each personality, we find ourselves assuming that only Melancholies are organized (although Cholerics can be as well) and that only Cholerics can be strong leaders (although others can learn to be such).

Also, many of us can find areas of our lives in which we've learned to act in a certain way, regardless of our natural tendency in the situation. In short, to discover our true personality, we must learn to distinguish between the *natural self* and the *trained self.* When we don't, we leave ourselves in a position of operating in a personality that is not really our own. In doing so, we put on a mask that hides our true personality, projects a false one, and ultimately wears us out.

So What about Me?

By now you've probably begun to recognize yourself and others in the descriptions you've read. It doesn't take long before we begin to get an idea of which personality we're most like. But before we begin to analyze our spouse's personality, it's important to take a look at ourselves.

To determine exactly what blend of personality you are, use the profile questionnaire below. In each row of four words, place an X in front of the word (or words) that most often applies to you. Continue through all forty lines. If you're not sure which word most applies to you, ask your spouse or a friend to help you. Use the word definitions in appendix B for the most accurate results.

Personality Profile Questionnaire

Strengths

1	__ Adventurous	__ Adaptable	__ Animated	__ Analytical
2	__ Persistent	__ Playful	__ Persuasive	__ Peaceful
3	__ Submissive	__ Self-sacrificing	__ Sociable	__ Strong-willed
4	__ Considerate	__ Controlled	__ Competitive	__ Convincing
5	__ Refreshing	__ Respectful	__ Reserved	__ Resourceful
6	__ Satisfied	__ Sensitive	__ Self-reliant	__ Spirited
7	__ Planner	__ Patient	__ Positive	__ Promoter
8	__ Sure	__ Spontaneous	__ Scheduled	__ Shy
9	__ Orderly	__ Obliging	__ Outspoken	__ Optimistic
10	__ Friendly	__ Faithful	__ Funny	__ Forceful

25

11	__ Daring	__ Delightful	__ Diplomatic	__ Detailed
12	__ Cheerful	__ Consistent	__ Cultured	__ Confident
13	__ Idealistic	__ Independent	__ Inoffensive	__ Inspiring
14	__ Demonstrative	__ Decisive	__ Dry humor	__ Deep
15	__ Mediator	__ Musical	__ Mover	__ Mixes easily
16	__ Thoughtful	__ Tenacious	__ Talker	__ Tolerant
17	__ Listener	__ Loyal	__ Leader	__ Lively
18	__ Contented	__ Chief	__ Chart maker	__ Cute
19	__ Perfectionist	__ Pleasant	__ Productive	__ Popular
20	__ Bouncy	__ Bold	__ Behaved	__ Balanced

Weaknesses

21	__ Blank	__ Bashful	__ Brassy	__ Bossy
22	__ Undisciplined	__ Unsympathetic	__ Unenthusiastic	__ Unforgiving
23	__ Reticent	__ Resentful	__ Resistant	__ Repetitious
24	__ Fussy	__ Fearful	__ Forgetful	__ Frank
25	__ Impatient	__ Insecure	__ Indecisive	__ Interrupts
26	__ Unpopular	__ Uninvolved	__ Unpredictable	__ Unaffectionate
27	__ Headstrong	__ Haphazard	__ Hard to please	__ Hesitant
28	__ Plain	__ Pessimistic	__ Proud	__ Permissive
29	__ Angered easily	__ Aimless	__ Argumentative	__ Alienated
30	__ Naïve	__ Negative attitude	__ Nervy	__ Nonchalant
31	__ Worrier	__ Withdrawn	__ Workaholic	__ Wants credit
32	__ Too sensitive	__ Tactless	__ Timid	__ Talkative
33	__ Doubtful	__ Disorganized	__ Domineering	__ Depressed
34	__ Inconsistent	__ Introvert	__ Intolerant	__ Indifferent
35	__ Messy	__ Moody	__ Mumbles	__ Manipulative
36	__ Slow	__ Stubborn	__ Show-off	__ Skeptical
37	__ Loner	__ Lord over others	__ Lazy	__ Loud
38	__ Sluggish	__ Suspicious	__ Short-tempered	__ Scatterbrained
39	__ Revengeful	__ Restless	__ Reluctant	__ Rash
40	__ Compromising	__ Critical	__ Crafty	__ Changeable

Once you've completed the profile, transfer your answers to the scoring sheet that follows. Add up your total number of responses in each column and combine your totals from the strengths and weaknesses sections.

Personality Scoring Sheet

Strengths

Popular Sanguine	Powerful Choleric	Perfect Melancholy	Peaceful Phlegmatic
1 __ Animated	__ Adventurous	__ Analytical	__ Adaptable
2 __ Playful	__ Persuasive	__ Persistent	__ Peaceful
3 __ Sociable	__ Strong-willed	__ Self-sacrificing	__ Submissive
4 __ Convincing	__ Competitive	__ Considerate	__ Controlled
5 __ Refreshing	__ Resourceful	__ Respectful	__ Reserved
6 __ Spirited	__ Self-reliant	__ Sensitive	__ Satisfied
7 __ Positive	__ Promoter	__ Planner	__ Patient
8 __ Spontaneous	__ Sure	__ Scheduled	__ Shy
9 __ Optimistic	__ Outspoken	__ Orderly	__ Obliging
10 __ Funny	__ Forceful	__ Faithful	__ Friendly
11 __ Delightful	__ Daring	__ Detailed	__ Diplomatic
12 __ Cheerful	__ Confident	__ Cultured	__ Consistent
13 __ Inspiring	__ Independent	__ Idealistic	__ Inoffensive
14 __ Demonstrative	__ Decisive	__ Deep	__ Dry humor
15 __ Mixes easily	__ Mover	__ Musical	__ Mediator
16 __ Talker	__ Tenacious	__ Thoughtful	__ Tolerant
17 __ Lively	__ Leader	__ Loyal	__ Listener
18 __ Cute	__ Chief	__ Chart maker	__ Contented
19 __ Popular	__ Productive	__ Perfectionist	__ Pleasant
20 __ Bouncy	__ Bold	__ Behaved	__ Balanced

TOTAL—STRENGTHS

_____ _____ _____ _____

Weaknesses

Popular Sanguine	Powerful Choleric	Perfect Melancholy	Peaceful Phlegmatic
21 __ Brassy	__ Bossy	__ Bashful	__ Blank
22 __ Undisciplined	__ Unsympathetic	__ Unforgiving	__ Unenthusiastic

23	__ Repetitious	__ Resistant	__ Resentful	__ Reticent
24	__ Forgetful	__ Frank	__ Fussy	__ Fearful
25	__ Interrupts	__ Impatient	__ Insecure	__ Indecisive
26	__ Unpredictable	__ Unaffectionate	__ Unpopular	__ Uninvolved
27	__ Haphazard	__ Headstrong	__ Hard to please	__ Hesitant
28	__ Permissive	__ Proud	__ Pessimistic	__ Plain
29	__ Angered easily	__ Argumentative	__ Alienated	__ Aimless
30	__ Naïve	__ Nervy	__ Negative attitude	__ Nonchalant
31	__ Wants credit	__ Workaholic	__ Withdrawn	__ Worrier
32	__ Talkative	__ Tactless	__ Too sensitive	__ Timid
33	__ Disorganized	__ Domineering	__ Depressed	__ Doubtful
34	__ Inconsistent	__ Intolerant	__ Introvert	__ Indifferent
35	__ Messy	__ Manipulative	__ Moody	__ Mumbles
36	__ Show-off	__ Stubborn	__ Skeptical	__ Slow
37	__ Loud	__ Lord over others	__ Loner	__ Lazy
38	__ Scatterbrained	__ Short-tempered	__ Suspicious	__ Sluggish
39	__ Restless	__ Rash	__ Revengeful	__ Reluctant
40	__ Changeable	__ Crafty	__ Critical	__ Compromising

TOTAL—WEAKNESSES

_____   _____   _____   _____

COMBINED TOTALS

_____   _____   _____   _____

Now you're able to see your dominant personality type. You'll also see what combination of personalities you are. If, for example, your score is 35 in Powerful Choleric strengths and weaknesses, there's really little doubt. You're nearly all Powerful Choleric. But if your score is, for example, 16 in Powerful Choleric, 14 in Melancholy, and 5 in each of the others, you're a Powerful Choleric with a strong Perfect Melancholy personality also.

You'll find an extra copy of this test and scoring sheet in appendix C so that both you and your spouse can identify your personality type.

A New Set of Characters

After coming to CLASS (Christian Leaders, Authors, & Speakers Seminars) and learning about the personalities, a woman named Suzie came up to me and excitedly said, "You can use this information anywhere. In marriage, family, and business!" As a hair stylist, Suzie dealt with people of all kinds every day, and she had never before understood their differences. She knew some were "strange," but she didn't know why!

Suzie later explained that learning the personalities allowed her to understand how her customers "processed" information. Once she understood where people were coming from, she was able to care for them in a completely different way. Being a Choleric, Suzie was fast, cared only about the bottom line, and wanted to get on with it. But she learned to slow down and explain in detail for the Melancholy and to help make the Phlegmatics feel secure by showing and telling them how they could manage their hair. Knowing they would show up late with a story to tell, she would tell Sanguines their appointment was fifteen minutes earlier than it really was so that she stayed on track for the rest of the day. She also noted that a boring hairdo was out of the question for the Sanguine; it had to be fun and different!

As we all become aware of the personalities, everyone we meet in life will be a learning experience. Look at your life as a TV situation comedy. You are the scriptwriter, and each day you get to choose a new cast of characters. As you read some real-life stories in this book, you will begin to spot personality differences in your own life. Soon you will be writing your own comedies!

Once we understand these inborn personalities, we can see why even people from the same family don't function the same way. We have our own mix of thirty thousand genes, but narrowing the system down to four types makes it much easier for us to grasp and to use in getting along with those other people who seem nothing like us. In the next chapter, we will take a special look at why understanding the four personalities matters in marriage.

two

THE RHYTHM OF A MORAL MARRIAGE

Do Personalities Make a Difference?

In a recent article in the *Desert Sun* newspaper, Gerald Ford had this to say about his more than fifty-year marriage to Betty: "I am optimistic in my marriage, and it has paid off with fifty years of wonderful happiness. We have basically the same ideology. We have an understanding of our different personalities so that we are able to reconcile our differences in a responsible way."

Ford's words remind us that when we don't understand the personalities, we can't understand each other and work out our differences. We may love each other *emotionally* when we get married without really *knowing* how the other person thinks. But as the passion dims and we face the routine of everyday life, we need a method of understanding that goes beyond emotion. Without that understanding, communication breaks down, and we either get angry or we freeze up and don't talk at all. These natural responses leave both spouses feeling dissatisfied and alone.

Fortunately, God has blessed us with the ability to learn about the different personalities. This understanding can save couples from a great deal of heartache and prevent the frustrations of a seesaw marriage.

The Seesaw Marriage

When I was a child, we had simple toys that involved some type of action or creativity. There was no TV to watch, no video games where we could blow up the world by pressing a button. My friend Peggy had a swing set with a seesaw attached. It didn't take much thinking to realize that we couldn't both be on the up end of the seesaw at the same time. When one was up, the other was down. The skill in this game was to achieve a balance. But this didn't last long because as soon as one of us would move independently, the balance was lost. One of us was *up* again, and the other was *down.*

This game is a lot like marriage. One of us is up, the other is down, and we keep teetering back and forth, seldom maintaining a balance for long. The moments of harmony give us hope—we do love each other—but just one thoughtless comment from our partner can push us down. Then we feel down and hurt, while the one that did the pushing has a twinge of guilt.

These negative feelings of hurt and guilt wipe out passion and make love questionable. We begin to think, "Let's forget trying to make this marriage work. Other people seem to like me just the way I am. Why am I the one who has to do all the changing?" Eventually we get sick of being on the down side and decide to jump off. But we don't realize how hard the crash will be for our spouse. As they pick themselves up, hurting from the bruised ego, they say, "That's it! I'm not playing this game ever again."

The ups and downs of marriage are difficult enough, but when neither one of us will even play the game there is little hope. Understanding each other's personalities will give you a new game

31

plan, a game full of hope with a prize of peace. No more ups and downs, no pushing each other off, no more hurts and guilt. Instead, you can keep your marriage in balance, give away the seesaw, and play the rewarding game of love.

Miserable Marriages Can Make You Sick

Unfortunately, many people do not realize how important it is to work at balancing their "marital seesaw." Not only does working toward marital balance bring joy to a relationship, it also saves individuals from a lot of pain.

On February 12, 2001, the Life section of *USA Today* proclaimed, "Miserable Marriages Can Make You Sick." I perked right up when I saw that headline, because I knew those words were true from thirty years of working with mixed-up marriages and almost fifty years of my own. As I read the article, I saw quotes from several recent studies of married people. They all came to similar conclusions: A happy marriage protects women from strokes and heart attacks after menopause, when the risk naturally rises sharply. Conversely, a miserable marriage can do us in! Ultrasound scans of carotid arteries and the aorta showed significant differences in those women who reported happy marriages versus those who were miserable with their mate.

The experts suggested that when women think they are pushing away their hurts, their body actually takes the pain and reacts negatively. Any conflict in marriage takes its toll by raising our blood pressure. And further symptoms of a bad marriage include weight gain, lack of exercise, and indifference to looks and grooming. According to findings by Ohio State University psychologist Janice Kiecolt-Glaser, verbal conflict upsets women more than men and makes them sick more often because "women are much more physically responsive to interactions in marriage. They remember the arguments in detail."

There is no simple answer to stress in marriage, but as Fred and I have worked with couples, we have found positive changes in those who realize, perhaps for the first time, that people are born with their personality. Miserable marriages can be prevented when these couples learn about the personalities, and when they discover that they aren't out to get each other and that just because they are different doesn't make either one of them wrong.

A Good Marriage Is Good for You

If miserable marriages make you sick, does a good marriage make you well? Or would we all be happier living alone forever? At a recent seminar, I quoted an article that said, "Married people live longer than singles." As I took a breath, a wiseguy yelled, "We don't really live longer. It just *seems* longer."

After ten years of research, the authors of a new book called *The Case for Marriage* have statistically proven that contrary to this man's opinion, married couples do live longer, happier, and healthier lives. In amassing statistics on longevity, they found that men who are forty-eight years old and married have a 90 percent chance of still being alive at sixty-five. In single or divorced men, only about six out of ten will pass sixty-five. And contrary to the myth that divorce brings individuals relief and happiness, only 18 percent of the divorced people in their study said they were happy. "They are more likely to be poor, have more problems with depression and substance abuse. Unless there is violence or extreme levels of conflict in the home, there are no benefits to children, only risks."[1]

Authors Linda J. Waite and Maggie Gallagher point out that our country has bought the lie that divorce is no problem and that it doesn't hurt children. We have deluded ourselves to the point that we are on the verge of a "post-marriage culture" where we don't

33

1. Linda J. Waite and Maggie Gallagher, *The Case for Marriage: Why Married People Are Happier, Healthier, and Better Off Financially* (New York: Doubleday, 2000).

believe marriage brings benefits to the individuals and society at large. The results of Gallagher and Waite's study are not surprising, given the plan that God has laid out for us in his Scripture. He created us to enjoy committed marriage, and when we violate God's best plan for the family, it will not have positive results.

Knowing that divorce is not a happy (or healthy!) option, what can we do to get more pleasure from our marriage?

My aim in writing about the personalities is to give you some simple, even enjoyable, tools that you can use to lighten up your life together and bring some new sparkle back into your relationship. I've been on both sides of marital understanding and want to help you brighten up your marriage, keep you healthy, and make the whole process fun.

Unrealistic Expectations

All of us have some expectations of what marriage will be like. We first get these ideas from watching our parents relate and then build on them by reading and viewing TV. In the distant past, we watched the Ozzie and Harriet marriage pattern and then carried those expectations into our households. Today's romantic movies frequently glorify the romantic feelings of love but rarely depict the work and careful thinking that marriage requires. With such notions of marriage, our expectations and optimism become unrealistic.

A Rocky Start

Phlegmatic Sarah came into marriage from a normal, balanced, low-key family. Members spoke nicely to each other, and they had good manners at the table and in public. She met Robert shortly after college and was struck by his powerful command of any situation. When he entered a room people "sat up and took notice," as her mother noted when he first came to visit.

Because of the calm in her home, Sarah was fascinated by the differences in Robert. When she learned that he had lived in a dysfunctional home, she was not concerned. Instead, she remained optimistic about his ability to separate himself from the emotional trauma he and his siblings had suffered. He gave her new energy, but after a day out with him, she was exhausted.

Robert didn't bring her to meet his family until they were engaged. As she learned later, he had threatened them to be on good behavior. They seemed to be an affable group, although certainly much more noisy than her family. Her expectations of a happy marriage made her blind to the turmoil surging around his family.

Once they settled into marriage, as so often happens, Robert's strengths were carried to extremes and soon became weaknesses. His quick control became overbearing and bossy. His loud commanding voice turned into yelling, and his charm became manipulation. Soon, his quick way with words became crude. Sarah learned not to disagree with Robert because almost anything could start a fight. Peace-loving Sarah soon wondered what she had married into.

Sarah later reflected that she should have been more realistic about the impact Robert's family life had had on him. The years of tension leading to his parents' near-divorce had a deep effect on the children. She now realizes that her harmonious home life made her naïve to the results of living in an embittered home.

She soon found that yelling and screaming were a part of his everyday life. Curt words and rebellious attitudes rarely led to healthy family time, and no matter how hard he tried not to emulate something bad, it was inevitable that he would take on some of the attributes he had seen demonstrated by his parents.

After ten years of marriage, Sarah now sees how those years have penetrated Robert's inner being, regardless of his ability to suppress it. No matter how much he may try not to, Robert will sometimes take on his mother's rebellious nature and "shoot-from-the-hip" responses when asked to do something that may not instantly seem accommodating to him.

Obviously Sarah and Robert's marriage was rocky from the start, turning out to be far different from Sarah's rosy expectations. It was only after learning to understand his Choleric personality that Sarah eventually learned how to respond to him in a healthy way, allowing the storms to pass so that their marriage could remain on solid ground.

Environment Matters Too

Sarah and Robert's example teaches us another important lesson as well: We are born with a personality type (heredity), but a negative background (environmental) can turn the strengths into weaknesses. What parents demonstrate in their homes will set the stage for success or failure in their children's marriages. Adults reflect what they experienced in their childhood home, even if they realize it was wrong. And when couples come from very different family backgrounds, they often carry two very different sets of expectations into their marriage, resulting in frequent conflict and disillusionment.

Is there any hope for a contentious marriage like this? First, an understanding of the personalities takes the pressure off. Understanding our spouse's personality and past helps us to form more realistic expectations of our marriage. It also leads to important revelations: "You mean you're not out to get me? You don't spend all night planning ways to ruin my life?" When we see we were both born with our personality, we can face our weaknesses, admit they are detractors in our progress, and determine to change.

Some of us can change to a certain extent by our own power, but most of us after years of negative behavior need a miracle! Just trying to be good doesn't work. We need to ask the Lord Jesus to come into our life and do what we can't do. Once the Holy

Spirit enlivens us, it's like being filled at the gas pump. We have new energy and vigor.

Sarah and Robert's experience beautifully illustrates this healing experience. It is by the grace of God and their understanding of the personalities that their marriage has been saved. Since Robert made Jesus his Lord, his actions have become more and more sanctified. And Sarah can now take a breath and let the storm pass, understanding that Robert is the way he is mostly because God created his personality type, but also because of the way he was raised. As a thoughtful and subdued Phlegmatic, Sarah has also learned to recognize her own faults and appreciates the learning curve her strong Choleric spouse offers her.

With new expectations and the blessing of God, Sarah now says, "I am appreciative of Robert's strength because it has helped me reach goals that I know I would not have achieved without a push. I am also very grateful for our knowledge of the different personality types. Without it we would not be as far in our relationship as we are now."

"Lord, Change Him!"

When we fail to appreciate the different personalities, we easily become convinced that our spouse's differences from us make them wrong. We tell ourselves he should change because he's wrong. All our friends agree, he's wrong. After telling our side of the story, the counselor and the pastor agree too: He's wrong.

When we prove our spouse to be wrong, we feel better, but he is still the same. He sees no reason to change, because he has no use for our friend's opinion, and he refuses to go see the pastor or counselor. "What could they possibly tell us about our marriage? They don't live with us!" He waits for us to see that the fault lies with us. We remain civil to him, knowing that's what God would want of us, and rest in the assurance that our prayer group is diligently praying, "Lord, change him."

Does this scenario sound familiar? Are you still in God's waiting room, expecting any moment that the Lord will open the door, push your husband through, and say, "I've changed him"? Many of us spend our entire marriage waiting for the other person to change. But when couples spend their entire marriage simply hoping that someday their spouse will change, they live unfulfilled lives.

Trish, a bright, vivacious, and cheerful Sanguine wrote me her story of being married to a solid, intellectual, successful dentist. As a Perfect Melancholy, his biggest thrill in life was taking the braces off a teenage girl and hearing her say "WOW!"

Trish and Craig clearly had opposite personalities, and they spent twenty years of their marriage striving to change each other, expectantly and painfully waiting for each other to change. Craig was waiting for Trish to become more serious, purposeful, and thorough. He desired more perfection with Trish's home bookkeeping, and he would always say, "Whatever you do, don't commit me to any social schedule." Trish, on the other hand, was looking forward to his becoming more spontaneous, cheerful, peppy, and enthusiastic. She wanted him to be ever-ready to talk with her at great length or get together with friends and other families for fun.

Their marital conflict centered on the fact that Craig wanted Trish to do things his Melancholy way, right and perfect, while she was waiting for him to do things her Sanguine way, the fun, talkative, creative way. Trish responded to this conflict by ignoring Craig and stuffing her angry feelings inside. She often wondered why she was so tired, not realizing that she was depressed from failing to understand her own feelings and Craig's different personality.

Fortunately, these two did not continue in this frustrating waiting room forever. Trish read *Personality Plus* and began to understand the principles of the four personalities. When she saw in the paper that Fred and I were coming to their area to speak, she was excited to attend. But she didn't ask Craig to go because he never wanted to waste time on seminars that might touch on emotions. "That stuff is for women," was sure to be his reply.

But that night was different. As Trish prepared to leave, Craig asked where she was going. "To a Personality Plus seminar where this couple is going to show us how to get along with difficult people," she answered, shutting her mouth before adding, "like you."

"He must have been really bored that night," Trish told me later, "because he said right off, 'I'll go with you.'"

I remember meeting them that night. Craig told us how he had studied Hippocrates in dental school but had never applied the information to himself. (How typical of most of us.) Both Trish and Craig returned the next day, and he took detailed notes while she smiled and laughed. By the end of the day Craig was smiling and laughing too, and Trish began jotting down a few notes herself.

Over the years, as we have kept in touch with both Trish and Craig, they have changed their attitudes and behavior patterns. Craig is no longer waiting for Trish to grow up and become serious. He realizes that what made her attractive to him in the first place was her bubbly personality that drew people to her. He knows that he lacks her ease with people and is only comfortable socially when she is at his side. He has also learned that he shouldn't expect her to do the bookkeeping and then complain when it isn't done on time. To his delight, as he has lightened her load, she has become more responsible.

Trish has come to appreciate Craig's Melancholy thoughtfulness and attention to detail. She recognizes her need for his calming personality and has stopped trying to change him into a spontaneous and carefree person. Both she and Craig have come to see the amazing truth that when one of them makes positive changes, the other usually responds!

Like Trish and Craig, we will go to odd extremes to change our spouse when we don't understand his or her personality. We think, "If only she could be like me," or "I know I'll change him!"

39

Trish has taken our Personality Plus training and now shares her experience with others. She no longer prays, "Lord, change him," but instead asks, "Lord, keep changing me!"

God's Garden

When I first met Amy she was attending one of my personality workshops at Anaheim Convention Center. She came bouncing up to see me, and as she talked I could see her Sanguine humor and her Choleric controlling gestures. She was so excited to learn about the personalities and to know that just because her husband was different didn't make him wrong. They had been married seven years at that time and had four daughters, ages one, three, five, and seven.

"While I was sitting here today, God whispered in my ear." Amy was wide-eyed and pointing at her ear. "He said, 'Be still and know that I am God. Stop trying to control where you are to go next. Listen, for I have much to teach you.'" From that day on, Amy came to listen any time I spoke in Southern California and brought me roses from her garden. She read each personality book as it came out, and her whole family began to change without her forcing them to do so.

As she reflects on the early years of her marriage, Amy remembers times when her husband, Pete, would try to "calm her down" and change her light and fun personality into a serious one. "When I tried to make those changes," she remembers, "I was not as fun anymore and felt that I was wearing a mask to change the real me. But I wanted to make peace at any price." Amy would also try to change Pete. In his serious moments, she would tell him to lighten up and enjoy life. And so he too would feel uncomfortable, wearing a light and cheery mask when he was somewhat depressed. The more Amy told him to cheer up, the sadder he got.

Amy would pack the girls up in the van and drive through Pete's auto repair shop, waving and playing music, trying to "Cheer up Dad and the mechanics!" Now she laughs at those days and asks herself, "What was I thinking?"

Their pattern of wearing masks to please each other was wrong for both of them. But when God gave them the gift of understanding the personalities, Amy and Pete were able to go before God, ask him to reveal their weaknesses, and then let him mold them into the God-given temperament they were born to have.

Today Amy and Pete work together full time in their family business. Many of their customers compliment their peaceful marriage and ask how they can work and live together in perfect harmony. Amy smiles and tells them that understanding their personalities has made all the difference.

Just like the many colored roses Amy has brought to me from her garden, different personalities offer a unique contribution to the "bouquet" of marriage. As Amy once put it, "God made us to fill in our partner's weaknesses, not to wear ourselves out trying to change that other person."

Creative Combinations

One of the most hopeful principles of the personalities is that we fall in love with the opposite strengths. But this also means we go home to live with the opposite weaknesses. Did God make a big mistake here? Should he have paired us up with sweet, compatible people who would always see things our way? It sounds peaceful, doesn't it? But this stressless life just doesn't seem to happen.

I have found in my many years of working with couples that our natural choice is to marry someone who is opposite and who fills in our blank spaces. The quiet, introspective, organized Melancholy marries the chatty, fun-loving, exciting Sanguine. The bold, controlling, independent Choleric marries the peaceful, submissive, unexcitable Phlegmatic. In these combinations, each partner's strengths fill in the other's weaknesses. Wasn't it clever of God to plan it this way?

God is more creative and exciting than we give him credit for. We so often think of him as some legalistic father figure who only knows us when we are in church. But in reality God created us, and he gave us the personality he wanted for us. He also gave us a desire for someone who is different and who fills in our gaps so that together we make a whole. Fred and I have found this to be true in our marriage. Though we have similar Choleric tendencies to get life under control, we are also opposites in that he is a Melancholy while I am a Sanguine. He wants everything in order, balanced, and on time, but my Sanguine nature wants to enjoy life. Why live in gloom?

As I look back on raising our children, I realize we balanced each other out. Think of having two of Fred. What a serious, perfectionistic life with no laughs that would be. Then again, the laughs of two Sanguine parents might not be so funny if the children were late for school each day and had no lunches.

As we consider these factors, Fred and I are grateful for the differences in our personalities. In the game of life, I knock over the puzzle and Fred picks up the pieces. He doesn't even complain anymore, and occasionally he even laughs at the amusing way I court disaster.

Because couples do tend to marry their opposite personality, the four personality sections in part 2 will emphasize the Sanguine/Melancholy and the Choleric/ Phlegmatic combinations. In our years of experience, these combinations have the most difficulty until they find the reason why. But once they see they're not out to get each other, they relax and enjoy the strengths of the opposite personality

Using the personalities to understand your marriage will be a fun experience for both of you together. Take the Personality Profile, add up your scores, and see where you both come out. Together, you can learn to appreciate your marriage's special combination.

It Takes All Four

One of the individuals who has attended our Personality Training workshop is Dr. Jerry Ozee. While at the workshop, a new idea came to his mind that the structure of our human heart has similarities to the four basic personalities. "How natural," Jerry thought. "Hippocrates was a physician. He knew the human body as well as the temperament patterns." When Jerry came up to share this conclusion with me, I asked him to put it in writing so that we might all see this correlation.

"I find it curious," he wrote, "to think that the God who created humanity, which expresses four basic personalities, also put within that creation a precious heart, which he addresses directly and repeatedly in his instructions to us in his Word." Jerry went on to point out that within our heart there are four chambers. Two of these are receiving chambers (auricles), corresponding to the two introverted, introspective personalities, Melancholy and Phlegmatic. The other two are pumping chambers (ventricles), much like the extroverted, driven, high-energy personalities, Sanguine and Choleric.

Just as all four heart chambers are essential to a balanced, well-functioning circulatory system, and therefore to biological life itself, the four personalities are essential to a well-balanced human condition. A combination of different personalities sustains the health and prosperity of your family, our church, our country, and ultimately the entire human race.

Jerry's clever analogy shows us that just like the beating of our hearts, a steady rhythm of give and take is at the heart of every good marriage.

three

WHEN CYMBALS CRASH

Hot Conflicts in Marriage

Spending money. Disciplining kids. Planning a vacation. These decisions can cause conflict for even the most dedicated of married couples. But when neither spouse understands the personality of the other, these conflicts can magnify into marriage disasters!

Now that we have learned about the different personalities in marriage relationships, we begin to understand the potential for disastrous conflicts. Popular Sanguines want to make life spontaneous and fun, but the Perfect Melancholies they often marry want life to be serious and in order. For the Powerful Choleric, it is important to accomplish something and keep life under control. But their Peaceful Phlegmatic spouse simply wants life to be calm and serene. These deep differences affect every area of marriage—and when couples do not understand each other's perspective, trouble brews.

I have found that certain topics naturally seem to bring out the differences in spouses' personalities. These "hot topics" can create tension and frustration that eat away at a couple's love. But when spouses learn to look at these topics through each other's eyes, calming the troubled waters becomes a much easier task.

Let's take a look at some of these "hot conflicts" and learn how the different personalities tend to deal with them.

Finances

It is not surprising that money causes frequent disagreements in marriage, especially when two different personalities are involved. Spouses work hard to earn the money they share, and they each have their preferences for how it should be spent.

The carefree Sanguine, whose idea of balancing the checkbook is to write a check and see if it bounces, tends to spend money on anything that sounds fun. The short-term satisfaction of a spontaneous purchase is far more gratifying to them than the patient saving toward a long-term goal. Melancholies, by contrast, are very detailed and want to investigate matters fully before any investment is made. When the Choleric sets her mind on a financial goal, there is no stopping her. This is the person who will shift her savings and investments frequently, just to get the best deal and feel that she is controlling her money. By contrast, Phlegmatic spouses just hope someone else will take care of the budget. They may just save a bundle of money and never get around to buying the item they were saving for!

The Check's in the Mail and the Deposit's . . . Somewhere

My friend Rhonda is a bright and engaging Sanguine, a CLASS graduate, and an author with published articles in major Christian periodicals. Her husband, Rick, is a Melancholy, introverted and orderly. Not surprisingly, he likes to balance the checkbook each month to see if their record matches the amount of money on their bank statement. Rhonda is happy if she can find the checkbook! And if the bank says they have less money than the checkbook says, then the bank obviously made a mistake. "Why worry about it?" she says. "Let's go out for pizza!"

It didn't take Rhonda long to realize that her husband is very pessimistic when it comes to money. As she once said, "His gloomy outlook would do Eeyore proud!" He not only sees the glass half empty, but he's convinced that the glass leaks and that someone will probably come along and siphon the rest of it away. He also has some strong Choleric tendencies and likes to have things done his own way.

Rhonda, on the other hand, has always been the poster child for Sanguine. She's talkative, disorganized, and optimistic when it comes to finances. She sees the glass half full, with more on the way. She told me, "When life hands me lemons, I don't make lemonade; I whip up a lemon chiffon cake and invite the neighbors over!"

Rick learned early about Rhonda's Sanguine approach to financial management (as if Sanguines have an approach to financial management!). During her sophomore year in college, she bounced a check for her second semester dorm fees and was shocked when the bank told her there was no money to cover the costs. Rick calmly offered to figure out the problem, which she thought was an excellent idea. She just knew that he would find the bank's error, and she would be vindicated. So, with a tearful sniff, she hurried to her dorm room to retrieve her bank statements and checkbook. She handed him the pile and watched in amazement as his engineer's brain started to short-circuit right there in the middle of the student lounge.

"None of these statements are even opened," he choked. "You haven't balanced your checkbook since September?"

"No," she explained patiently. "Why bother? I knew the money was there."

In the end, Rick discovered that her check had bounced because of a tiny mistake in subtraction four months earlier. Rick hoped she had learned her lesson about keeping detailed records. But just a few days later, Rhonda received a one-hundred-dollar scholarship, which was exactly what she needed to cover the check.

True to her Sanguine nature, she saw the situation as a good opportunity for Rick to learn about God's provision.

As they now approach their twentieth anniversary, Rhonda sees Rick as the weighted string that keeps her Sanguine balloon from floating away. She now explains the three financial lessons they've learned: "One, every balloon needs a string, or it will float away into oblivion without accomplishing much of anything. Two, string is more interesting and a lot more fun if it has a balloon attached to one end. And three, never ask a Sanguine to balance the checkbook."

Rhonda and Rick's story is easy to laugh at—but in real life, financial conflicts can break up marriages. Learning to appreciate and balance our spouse's view of money may be a challenge, but it will also keep us from the financial extremes of hoarding or mindless spending.

Social Activities

Because some of the personalities love activity and people, while others prefer quietness and solitude, a couple's social calendar can be quite a source of contention. Melancholies and Phlegmatics are content to spend time alone, enjoying low-energy activities or thoughtful discussions with a quiet group of friends. But to Sanguines and Cholerics, this is no social event at all! The Choleric spouse enjoys big or small events, as long as they are in charge of it all. Sanguines feel stifled by planned activities, but love spontaneous gatherings with lots of people and lots of lighthearted fun.

When it comes to social activities, many personality combinations can cause problems. While Sanguines delight in having many social events to attend, Melancholies find themselves exhausted by all the activity. The Melancholy's quiet conversations, however, may put the Sanguine spouse to sleep. Phlegmatics will be easy to please in social activities, but their spouse may grow frustrated with their lack of enthusiasm for special events. And when the Sanguine's spontaneous fun interferes with a Choleric's planned activities, watch out! With all these different social interests, it's a wonder some couples manage to do any social activities together at all!

But no matter what personality combination you and your spouse share, communicating about each other's wants and needs can bring you to a compromise that keeps you both satisfied.

Save the Last Dance

Ellen is a delightful Sanguine who loves being surrounded by people and explains, "I really need to socialize. I enjoy getting out of the country and going to the city for an elegant dinner or a picnic in the park." Her husband, Bill, on the other hand, is a powerful Choleric who thrives on "being his own person" and takes charge of every situation.

While Ellen stayed home and was in charge of running the family farm, Bill's work sent him out of town every Sunday through Friday. This caused constant friction between the two because once Bill arrived home, he wanted to reestablish his role as the one in charge. Ellen would begrudge his attempt, but Bill would inevitably end up being the boss.

Ellen yearned for companionship and always looked forward to the weekend when her husband was home. She dreamed of romantic dinners and going to the theater, while her husband yearned for home-cooked meals and peace and quiet on the farm after a week on the road. As a Sanguine, Ellen was always looking for approval, so she never felt secure enough to insist on changing Bill's weekend plans. So once again they would stay home and do what Bill wanted to do, just the way he wanted to do it.

Finally, Ellen reached a point where she could no longer squelch her Sanguine need for fun and decided to address her husband about the differences in their relationship. After much talk and a little persuasion on Ellen's part, they finally reached a compromise: They'd split the weekends and alternate between his social plans and hers.

The farm offered little to no social activity for Ellen, so when a Christmas party invitation was extended, she jumped on the opportunity without consulting her husband. The mere thought of a social setting was so exciting to Ellen that it never entered her mind that it wasn't her weekend to choose the couple's activity.

As the days passed, her excitement mounted. She planned what she would wear and how she would explain the party to Bill. "I know," thought Ellen. "I'll surprise him! Everyone loves surprises." She waited until the day of the party to tell him of the plans and tried the charming Sanguine buildup before dropping the bomb. "There will be dancing with live music, chatting with friends and neighbors, and lots of Christmas cheer among all the holiday finery. You'll just love it!" Much to her disappointment, Choleric Bill didn't react positively to the surprise. However, he gave in and dressed for the party despite his feelings.

Ellen delighted in the twinkling lights, the Christmas music, and the romance that filled the air. She walked over to Bill, and with a provocative look she asked him to dance. His answer was a sharp, "No!"

Ellen was stunned and hurt, so for the next hour she completely ignored him. As she ate, sang Christmas carols, and talked among friends, she silently let Bill know that she didn't need him to have fun. Bill put up with her little game for just so long and then headed across the room, grabbed her by the elbow, and said, "We're leaving!"

After a stony ride home, Ellen sulked off to bed and pretended to be asleep when Bill returned from taking the baby-sitter home. Soon, Ellen broke into uncontrollable sobs as she began recalling the evening's events. "You used to love dancing, and you used to love me just the way I am."

Everything she had been keeping bottled up inside spilled out at that moment as she continued to reprimand him. "You could have pretended for one evening that you were enjoying the party with my friends. After all, I've done plenty for you that I haven't exactly enjoyed during the course of our marriage."

Bill sneered back, "Like what?"

Ellen replied, "Like taking care of the children and the farm all week long by myself and never having time for friends."

Shocked by this revelation, Bill said, "I thought you loved the farm!"

Ellen replied, "I do love the farm because I love you. And when you love someone the way I love you, you always save the last dance for them."

Bill grew silent. He looked down at the floor as he recollected the past and the woman he had fallen in love with. He realized that he had been trying to change all the personality traits he had once loved about her. With tears in his eyes, he looked back up at Ellen and said, " Honey, I'm a dancing fool!"

Sex

Blending opposite personalities in the area of sex takes some understanding and patience. But without the effort to understand each other's personalities, both spouses can be left feeling frustrated and hurt from their experiences in the bedroom.

Sanguines want sex to be spontaneous, creative, and fun. They are the ones who will suggest new ideas, and unusual places— "Why not on the dining room table for a change?" One Melancholy comment of, "I'm not ready yet," spoils the Sanguine spontaneity. "What's to get ready?"

The Melancholy prefers romantic sex with candles, flowers, and music to perfect the mood. One cute comment from the Sanguine can ruin the whole mood. To meet their expectations of perfection, they need time to prepare for sex, and their response to a spontaneous sexual advance from their spouse is usually, "But I didn't plan on it tonight."

Cholerics like quick, unplanned sex. They don't need much time, as long as it's frequent—"We've got ten minutes, let's go for it!" One hesitant look of "Not again" from the Phlegmatic can infuriate the Choleric—"But it's been two days!"

The Phlegmatic prefers "special event sex" on holidays, birthdays, and special occasions—"It's our anniversary, so we should get on with it." They need it to be slow, meaningful, and not too frequent. One "hurry up" from the Choleric can leave the Phlegmatic indifferent. "So where are we going?"

When we consider these differences, it's not hard to imagine that these different expectations can lead to conflict or hurt feelings in the bedroom. When we have opposite desires and needs for sex, each of us will be thinking, "Something's wrong here" or "This isn't what I expected." With such differences, it's amazing that any of us stay together! But what a difference it makes when we can talk about it.

Let's Talk about It

Many spouses never communicate about their sex life together. Instead of sharing their feelings, both the good and the bad, they avoid talking about physical intimacy and assume that what they have is "as good as it gets." Unfortunately, these couples miss an important opportunity to learn about each other's needs and expectations. And the result can be a sex life that is not satisfying to either spouse.

As with any area where different perspectives arise, it is important for couples to be compromising and considerate of their spouse's needs. The goofy Sanguine needs to remember the Melancholy's desire for a romantic atmosphere and make a special effort to avoid funny comments that hurt their spouse's feelings. On the other hand, the Melancholy needs to acknowledge that they are hurt easily and make some effort to be less serious about sex with a Sanguine spouse. Cholerics must remember that their need for frequent sex may be seen as selfish and uncaring to a Phlegmatic spouse. And Phlegmatics need to remember that the Choleric's impetuousness was part of what they fell in love with and to communicate honestly about when they are feeling like an impersonal sex object.

Talking to our spouse about sex may be awkward for us. But it is also important. The effort we make to understand our partner's sexual needs will be a wise investment. Not only will it give us greater confidence and understanding in our lovemaking style, but knowing how to fill our spouse's sexual needs will give us a deeper satisfaction when intimate.

Learning to Make Music Together

Rhonda and Rick learned quickly that their personality differences were going to crop up in the bedroom. As Rhonda learned, Melancholy Rick didn't stop being Melancholy just because the lights were low and the music was playing. And Rick discovered that Sanguine Rhonda remained playful and cute, even when she was in an amorous mood.

Because they were both Christians long before they met, they were committed to saving sex for marriage. For Rhonda, sex was something to look forward to, but something that would sort of "happen" once they were in the honeymoon suite. She is now thankful that Rick was a bit wiser. He knew that good sex doesn't just "happen," and he was determined to make this side of their marriage as wonderful as possible.

In typical Melancholy fashion, Rick proceeded in an orderly and logical way to read every Christian book he could find on the topic, and he insisted Rhonda read them too. She was cooperative, since she figured that the more knowledgeable they were, the better their chances for a healthy sex life and a satisfying marriage. Thus Rick's goal for a lifetime of sexual satisfaction became their goal together.

Even now, twenty years later, Rhonda appreciates the sweet things he did to ensure that she enjoyed their first act of intimacy as much as he knew he was going to. He put a great deal of thought into creating happy memories for her on the wedding night. Of course, once she got more comfortable with their intimacy, she eventually showed Melancholy Rick that his Sanguine sweetie had a few tricks of her own!

Fortunately, Rick's Melancholy desire for planned perfection prompted him to discuss physical intimacy with Rhonda before and after their honeymoon. This open communication has saved them from misunderstandings and conflicts over sex, and they can both enjoy each other's unique personalities in the act of love.

Eating Habits

The problem of weight control is one of the foremost topics in magazines and self-help articles, beauty books, and television shows. It seems everyone is unhappy with their weight. Magic trick diets and the "get thin quick" schemes abound. But just like other areas of life, the personalities look at food and exercise in completely different ways.

Sanguines eat because it's fun and because fattening foods taste good. They have trouble seeing the connection between a hot fudge sundae and a tight outfit. Food is often related to social activities and many spiritual Sanguine women get chubby from too many church potlucks. Their husbands are often gaunt, dour, godly men who could eat a sacrificial lamb and not gain an ounce!

Weight control is most difficult for Sanguines because they are undisciplined, lack follow-through, and always believe they will start a diet "next week." Sanguine women do best in programs like Jazzercise or weigh-ins and hope the process leads to weekly parties. They love buying fancy leotards and gym shoes with sequins—and if they diet at all, it is usually the latest fad diet that everyone is talking about. After all, they know the last diet didn't work, so why should they deprive themselves for nothing?

Melancholies are the opposite of undisciplined Sanguines. They love menu planning and they eat to enjoy a fine culinary experience. They tend not to overeat, except when they are struggling with depression. If they do overeat, they usually do it in secret,

53

becoming "closet drinkers and eaters." They don't want to show their poor habits to anyone because they are afraid people might think less of them.

The Melancholies don't go for miracle diets, but they will try balanced nutritious meals with the goal of taking off two pounds a month and keeping it off for life. They will work on their weight privately—and for them, this process is no party! They like to read books and articles on weight loss and are fascinated by calorie charts. They may even buy the little scales that measure ounces so they can talk endlessly about how many ounces they lose each week.

Cholerics are the fast-food, fast-action, and fast-loss leaders. They eat for the practical purpose of gaining sustenance, and once they are convinced they are getting fat, they get right down to business. They may join a fast-paced health spa and get to work. They have no time for books, lifelong programs, or parties in dancing leotards. Instead, they like a diet that will be close to a miracle, and they set goals based on how much they can lose in just a week. If they take diet pills guaranteed to take off five pounds in a day, they'll take two pills and expect to lose ten pounds.

If the first diet doesn't work quickly, they will give up and try another one. If two or three don't help, they may give up completely. "I did all the right things, and I didn't lose an ounce. So maybe God wants me chubby!" After all, the Cholerics don't have time to waste on a hopeless diet—they've got other projects to work on.

Phlegmatics will eat whenever and whatever food is easily accessible. They are slow starters, especially on things like diet and exercise. For them, exercise is especially difficult because it takes so much effort and shows so little results. They tend to put off their weight-loss program until "a better time," and they won't even consider attempting to diet during the holidays. Phlegmatics seldom make drastic changes to their diet. Like Scarlett O'Hara, they say, "Tomorrow is another day."

Phlegmatics would rather think about dieting than do it. So they may read about diets and exercise or ask other dieters what plan they are using. But unless they find a program that sounds exceptionally easy, they will likely continue looking and put off their diet yet another day.

Who's Counting Calories?

Jane is an overweight Phlegmatic who sees food as something God gave to us for enjoyment. She is an attractive lady and dresses well, but her husband, who eats food because it helps him function, wants a thin wife. As with most couples, she and her Choleric husband have different attitudes about weight and diet that have caused them some grief.

Jane began to gain weight several years ago, while her husband's weight remained exactly what the weight charts said it should be. The formula for his success included a regular pattern of daily exercise. But in order to fit this exercise into his busy schedule, he delegated many of the family and friend activities to Jane. He stayed on schedule, never missed a day of exercise, and never gained a pound. But Jane's relationships with family and friends got her off task, especially when the task was keeping her weight under control. To him, perfect weight was a very important part of reaching his goals. But for her, it was something she wanted to work on but did not find imperative.

As Jane continued gaining weight, the issue of diet and weight eventually became the albatross in their marriage. Her extra pounds grated on her husband. And knowing her husband's annoyance gave her many years of just-below-the-surface sorrow. His Choleric personality drove him to look for programs that would quickly take her weight off, and they spent hundreds of dollars trying to find something that would help her lose weight. But as a Phlegmatic, Jane's personality kept looking for some way to get around his strict regime.

Poor Jane! She had a lifetime of searching for the right plan and years of deep pain because of her husband's unspoken message that she was not thin enough to meet his standards. Her husband had not learned that the more you push the Phlegmatic, the more they dig in their heels and refuse to change! As Jane put it, "The watch-dog approach only made me want to rebel more and not get the weight off."

Then Jane and her husband became Christians and began to examine themselves instead of each other. This commitment didn't cause Jane to lose weight but it did change her attitude about losing weight. The Lord began to show each of them that everybody has weaknesses. And as Jane's husband recognized his own weaknesses in the areas of basketball games and overworking, he came to accept Jane's weaknesses in the area of food. Eventually, he shared this revelation with Jane and stopped being so watchful over every bite she ate.

Jane too experienced new revelations as she grew in her faith. She began to see that God had a plan for her that included her being able to have physical stamina. In a roundabout way, he began to reveal that her health could be harmed with extra weight, and that this would stand in the way of many of her life goals.

And so, with God's help, this couple came together on the issue of diet and weight loss. Jane still wishes her husband would accept her just the way she is, but he is coming closer. And as Jane recently shared with me, they are now to the point where their biggest diet conflict is over an occasional piece of blackberry pie!

Like Jane, many husbands and wives are hurt by their spouse's words about their weight. Because society puts so much emphasis on outward appearances, spouses often feel deeply saddened when they feel "too fat" or "too thin" for their spouse. As with all the hot topics, couples can benefit simply by taking the time to understand their spouse's personality and needs. Only as you come to appreciate the beauty of the inner person you fell in love with can you find a satisfactory way to work on your outside appearances together.

Work

Expectations about work can cause a great deal of conflict in marriage. Not only do couples sometimes disagree over the amount of work they should spend at jobs, but many husbands and wives have differences in attitude toward household chores as well.

Sanguines see work as a necessary evil, but will work hard at a job if there is a fun reward to be had. Of course, their spontaneous and fun-loving natures often prevent them from remaining at a serious task for very long. Melancholies by nature enjoy detailed work that requires thinking and concentration. They get distracted by projects requiring in-depth concentration and will neglect fun activities until they have finished the job to perfection.

Cholerics are the types who can easily become workaholics. Their drive and natural leadership abilities make them great in high-pressure and challenging situations, which can lead to promotions and benefits on the job. But their constant drive sometimes makes them lose focus on other areas of their life. In the home, Choleric spouses are hard workers, always eager to start and complete the next home improvement. Phlegmatics, by contrast, tend to put off work and procastinate when it comes to difficult tasks. They do enjoy people, and in the right job they are motivated to get the job done by their interaction with others. But without some encouragement and prodding, they often let projects slide by.

Understandably, a marriage between differing personalities can cause some conflict in the area of work. The spouse who enjoys fun and social activities will be hurt and frustrated by the spouse who gets distracted by their job. And the driven, controlling spouse tends to nag, while their more laid-back spouse feels tired and desperately wishes for a break from the hectic activity. To find a successful blend, most couples have to be willing to talk about and compromise on their job and household-project expectations.

"But I Just Finished the Last Project!"

One of the most difficult marriage combinations is the strong, work-driven Choleric wife who evaluates everyone by how much work they get done in a given day and the Phlegmatic man who feels he worked all day and needs to rest when he gets home. She usually meets him at the door with a list of things he must do immediately.

"Go pick Junior up at school. He's been standing on the corner for fifteen minutes already, waiting for you to come get him."

"Turn around and go back to the store!"

"Don't drop your jacket on the chair! What do you think we have closets for?"

"Set the table right now; the pastor's coming for dinner."

In situations like these, she sees him as lazy and he sees her as a slave driver. One Phlegmatic man told me he drives into the garage and sits in the car hoping he won't be discovered. "I relax and take a mental rest until I gather enough strength to go in and face her."

Another commented: "I go from work all day to work all night, and all I really want to do is rest!"

One has an answer. "I found this quiet park about halfway home. Each day I pull off the road and go to sleep. I can sleep just about anywhere. When I've had a good rest, I drive home and face the music. Of course, if she ever finds me there in the park, it's over."

From these brief examples you can see that each one is looking at their marriage from their own personality without understanding why they are different. She feels he is hopelessly lazy, and he thinks anyone who is such a compulsive worker must be crazy.

Choleric Sandy once told me, "I thought my husband was stupid. He couldn't seem to catch on to how to empty a dishwasher or clear the table without breaking a glass. I shoved him out of the kitchen one night and said, 'You're more trouble than you're worth.'" This scene didn't seem to bother her husband much, and one night as she was doing all the work, she saw him sitting in front of the TV, holding their youngest child. "They were so relaxed. And all of a sudden it hit me. Which one of us is the stupid one?"

These short examples may sound humorous when first read, but when they are being lived, they are not so fun. But believe it or not, different personalities can really work to the advantage of a couple's marriage! When it comes to work and household chores, the workhorses need the quiet relaxation that their laid-back spouses remind them to enjoy. And when nagging is limited to legitimate concerns about necessary work, the hard-to-motivate spouse can enjoy the satisfaction of completing a job. As with most areas of our life, our own weaknesses can be beautifully compensated by our partner's strengths.

Parenting

It's important for husbands and wives to understand that their different personalities will affect their parenting techniques. Most of us want to present a "unified front" when dealing with our children. But this can be difficult for husbands and wives who have different personalities. Unless parents learn how to deal with these differences, their children will take advantage of them by playing the parents against each other. Understanding your personality differences can also prevent hurt feelings or guilt that arise when one spouse seems to get along with a child better than the other.

The Popular Parent (Sanguine)

The Popular parent loves to have fun and thrives on an audience. She'll play games with her children and their friends, but since Sanguines get self-worth from the response of those around them, a disinterested group of children will cause the parent to turn off the charm. After all, why bother being cute and adorable if no one cares?

There's no worse punishment for the Sanguine parent than to be ignored by the family. Ever the showman, the Sanguine parent would like to have the starring role without being responsible for any of the hard work or details. Responsibility is not a plus in this parent's mind, and frequently the other personalities grow frustrated with their Sanguine spouse for "airheaded" mistakes that cause embarrassment to the family.

Sanguine spouses need special encouragement and understanding from their partner when they have an unresponsive and emotionally distant child. And even though it sometimes seems like the Sanguine parent is just another one of the kids, it's important to remember their unique ability to enjoy and interact with your children.

The Perfect Parent (Melancholy)

The Perfect parent is what all the others wish they were: clean, neat, organized, punctual, thoughtful, analytical, detail-conscious, compassionate, talented, dedicated, musical, patient, artistic, creative, poetic, sensitive, sincere, and steadfast. Could you ask for anything more? This parent takes on the raising of children as a serious lifetime project, and no other personality so totally dedicates itself to producing perfect children.

Melancholy parents may clash with a Sanguine who places higher priority on fun than on perfection. While the Melancholy is telling their child to finish their homework, their Sanguine spouse may be trying to distract the child with something more fun. These Sanguine efforts to win the child's approval often work but the result is that the Melancholy parent feels frustrated and unloved by the kids because they have to be the one who forces them back to work.

If you are married to a Melancholy spouse, you will need to remind them that not all children share their need for perfection—in fact, some kids may feel overwhelmed by such high expectations. But you should also be grateful for your Melancholy's attention to detail. It will probably save your family from disorder and many embarrassing moments.

The Powerful Parent (Choleric)

Because Powerful parents instantly become commander in chief in any situation, being in charge of the family seems a natural for them. All they have to do is line up the troops and give orders. It all sounds so simple. Cholerics believe that if everyone would only do things their way—immediately—we could all live happily ever after. The Choleric father is accustomed to giving firm orders in the business world without anyone second-guessing him, and he expects the same respect at home. A Choleric mother, often married to a Phlegmatic man who wouldn't dream of disagreeing with her, controls the family firmly, and her quick decisions are usually right.

Not only is such a home under control, but the Choleric parent can even make work out of leisure time. This individual doesn't like any rest and considers relaxing a sin to be avoided. One Powerful father took his children to Disneyland. He felt noble to be giving up his productive time to humor his family. He bought the tickets and let everyone know how much they cost. The man marched his children into Disneyland for a "fun-filled" day. After an hour, a cloudburst hit the area and his wife and children wanted to head for the car. "What do you think you're doing?" he asked. "We paid good money to get into this place, and we are not going to let a little rain spoil our fun. You will go on the rides and you will enjoy them. We are going to get our money's worth!"

When this man's Peaceful wife told me the story, it was both pitiful and hilarious. "Can you imagine having fun on a roller coaster in pouring-down rain when you can't see a foot in front of you and the children are crying to go home?" she asked. This Powerful man not only got his money's worth, he also achieved another triumph. The family never asked him to take them to Disneyland again!

If you are the spouse of a Choleric, it's important to tell them that getting their own way may not be the best way to reduce tension in the home. They need gentle (and maybe not-so-gentle) reminders that not all your children share their zesty drive for life. But you can also rejoice in having a spouse with a special knack for motivating the children for both learning and fun.

The Peaceful Parent (Phlegmatic)

Peaceful parents have the kind, low-key, relaxed, patient, sympathetic nature that we find so agreeable and acceptable in a father or mother. They don't argue or fight, they don't insist on high achievement, they roll with the punches, and they're never irrational or hysterical. What more could any child want? Many little ones would be glad to turn in their dramatic, emotional, Popular mother; their dictatorial, temperamental, Powerful father; or their critical, nit-picking Perfect parent for one Peaceful protector.

This easygoing parent has some shortcomings, though. Unless the Phlegmatic parent develops a set of guidelines for discipline and sticks to it, a Sanguine child may charm his way out of deserved consequences and a Choleric child will run the household. Peaceful parents must force themselves to invest energy into their relationships with their children, lest communication becomes nonexistent.

Not surprisingly, the easygoing attitude of a Phlegmatic parent may cause marital problems, especially with a hard-driven Choleric spouse. When Cholerics are rallying the troops for the next trip or project, they will be frustrated by the lack of assistance from their laid-back spouse. Phlegmatics, on the other hand, will grow annoyed with their Choleric spouse's need for continuous family projects and activities.

If you are married to a Phlegmatic, try to be understanding when they get tired out by busy children and family activities. However, you should also encourage them toward taking responsibility as a parent, or they may withdraw from your family's world. With the support and urging of a loving spouse, Phlegmatics are great parents who make your home a haven of peace from the bustling world.

Making It through the Hot Topics

Once you and your spouse have learned about the different personalities, you will find that handling the hot topics becomes much more manageable. Though it may not always be easy to reach a comfortable compromise, understanding your spouse's personality will give you greater incentive to meet their needs as well as your own.

In his perfect plan for you and your spouse, God will blend your personalities together for the better, even in the tough spots. Though it may not always feel like it, he did give you the spouse you have for a reason. The personality differences that cause the most conflicts are also the ones that keep you from going to the negative extremes of your personality.

Learning to work with a different personality not only allows you to grow as a caring individual, but the compromises you make will help you both live a more balanced life. Part 2 of this book gives you an in-depth look at each personality so you can effectively handle the hot topics together.

PART 2
Getting in Tune

Living with the Personalities

four

THE SONG OF THE SANGUINE

Sunshine, Lollipops, and Roses

Alana has a bubbly personality that is always attracting the attention of others. As she talks to family and friends, Alana frequently jokes that she is the favorite in the family. The typical message she leaves on her mother's answering machine is, "Hey, Mom, give your favorite daughter a call when you get home!"

Popular Sanguines have an innate desire for fun and games. Their cheerful attitude endears them to others, and they are happy as long as they can laugh and be loved. Since Sanguines always seem to have more fun than those around them, others flock to them. At the center of the party, they will bask in the attention by sharing an exaggerated story.

Sanguines don't like problems, conflict, or excessive work because they all crowd in on their time for fun. Because they seek approval for all that they do, they don't relate well to people who put them down, humiliate them in public, or make them feel stupid.

If you are a Sanguine, or you are married to a Sanguine, it's important to recognize this personality's unique characteristics.

The Dumb Blond

Sanguine Alana wrote me after a seminar to tell me how relieved she was to find out that there was a name for her besides "dumb blond." Her Melancholy parents had considered her some misfit, and for all of her life she had been struggling to be a Melancholy like them. Imagine a bright, chatty, hilarious Sanguine trying each day to be deep, quiet, thoughtful, and perfect. She has ended up confused and insecure   and so is everyone who tries to deal with her!

After reading *Personality Plus,* she began to see herself as a Popular Sanguine who wasn't crazy after all. For the first time, she realized that her personality didn't have to be like her parents and that there were other people who were just like her. In her letter, she expressed her delight and relief in learning that she was a Sanguine.

Unfortunately, some Sanguines are married to a spouse who simply doesn't understand their fun-loving ways. Instead of filling their emotional needs, their spouse may try to change them, telling them to "stop acting like a child" and "get some work done!" But unless a spouse learns how to meet the Sanguine emotional needs, they will be left with a very sad mate.

Sanguine Emotional Needs

The Sanguine needs are "gimme" needs. They want to have attention, approval, and affection   and they want to have it all the time. These sunny personalities also need to have frequent interaction and activity with people or they will start to feel bored with life. When these needs are met, the Sanguine personality can enjoy life without trying to constantly get their spouse's attention. The following list offers a few pointers for meeting the needs of a Sanguine spouse:

1. **Attention:** Sit down, look them in the eye, and listen. Don't interrupt, cut them off, look around the room, or

try to "fix it" when they are sharing a problem. They just want your attention.

2. **Approval:** Sanguines are desperate for approval. They don't think anyone appreciates what they have done. Don't say, "That would have been good if only . . ." When you correct them frequently, they think you are out to get them. Instead, make an effort to thank and praise them when a job has been well done.

3. **Affection:** Sanguines want to be loved. Think of a little child saying, "Daddy, please love me." The Sanguine has a beguiling, childlike appeal. Respond to it. "You're so pretty, bright, smart, talented, charming, witty, fun . . ." They can never get enough love.

4. **Activity:** Don't ignore your spouse's requests to "get out" or spend time with friends. The Sanguine starts to feel like an animal in a cage when they are not allowed frequent interaction with family and friends. Plan some special events for the two of you that gets you out of the house. Encourage your spouse's involvement in church and community events.

If you are a Sanguine yourself, try to remember that your emotional needs demand a lot of energy and time. A Melancholy or Phlegmatic spouse will have an especially difficult time with your need for constant conversation and activity. If you are always hanging around your spouse in order to seek their approval and affection, you are more likely to get an annoyed sigh than a hug and a compliment. Remind yourself that your spouse has needs too, and they may require that you give them some space for a while before you seek out another fun activity.

Instructions?

Sanguines are notorious for failing to read directions. They are so eager to get to the fun part that they take the shortest route to get there. Since detailed instructions get in the way of the fun, they just throw them away and hope for the best.

One Christmas, Sanguine Alana received a beautiful camera from her friends because they knew that she enjoyed photography. But months later, she still hadn't read the instructions or bothered to fill out the warranty card. She had figured out how to use the camera under the automatic pilot setting, but she still didn't have a clue how to use all the other wonderful features it provided.

She finally mentioned to one of her friends that she needed to have someone teach her about the camera's features. Her Choleric friend looked at her in disbelief and said, "Alana, it came with an instruction manual!"

In true Sanguine form, Alana responded, "What does that have to do with anything?"

If you are married to a Sanguine spouse, keep in mind that they will rarely bother with instructions. If your Sanguine mate tells you they want to learn a new hobby, you had better sign them up for a class where they can interact with other people. If you make the mistake of buying them a lengthy book about the subject, don't be surprised to find it accumulating dust on the shelf!

If It Isn't Fun, It Doesn't Get Done!

One of the other difficult areas for the Sanguine is keeping focused on the job at hand. The Sanguine mind jumps from one thought to another so quickly that on the way to one duty they forget where they were going. My Choleric daughter Lauren challenges herself by what she calls multitasking, doing many things at one time. But Sanguines are better off sticking to one task at a time. As a Sanguine friend of mine says about her cooking, "I only dare to turn on one burner at a time."

Sanguines don't like housework of any kind, especially those tasks that can't be seen and appreciated by casual observers. They tend to shove things in drawers when the doorbell rings and not find them again for weeks. Some things disappear into that great closet in the sky, never to be seen again. They just don't want to miss out on living because they're busy cleaning a house.

When Sanguines finally do get around to household chores, they never stick to a cleaning schedule   they get sidetracked too easily. They could be on their way to one room to vacuum, but while placing something in a drawer on the way, they decide that drawer needs to be cleaned out. By the end of the day, they've done several things that needed to be done for years but aren't noticeable, and the house still doesn't look completely clean. That's when Sanguines get depressed, feeling like they've wasted a whole day cleaning when they could have been out having fun. "Oh, what's the use!"

But a Sanguine spouse will make work fun when they do get around to working. So if you're married to a Sanguine, don't get too serious with the cleaning projects. And when they complete a task, make sure you encourage and praise them for a job well done.

My Best Friend

My daughter Marita is Sanguine/Choleric just like me. We both like to be in charge of the fun. Naturally, she married Melancholy Chuck. He is so deep and thoughtful that he could be the national poster boy for Melancholies.

One morning Marita overheard him talking introspectively to himself in the shower "Anyone who isn't at least a little bit depressed doesn't understand the gravity of life."

Marita rushed in and exclaimed, "That was a classic. May I use it?"

His momentary revelation of truth didn't seem exceptional to him, and he simply said, "If you like it, you can have it."

Had Chuck been Sanguine and someone wanted to quote him, his reaction would have been exuberant. "You want to quote me? Will I be in a book? A movie? I've got more stories! When will my words be published? Will it be out by Christmas?" Sanguines love attention and will grab at any opportunity.

If Marita didn't understand the personalities, her Sanguine spirit would be frequently crushed by his lack of enthusiasm for the fun she creates. Chuck's not being negative from his perspective, he's just being realistic from his Melancholy point of view. So Marita has learned to do what many Sanguines do— make lots of Sanguine friends!

Once when Marita was speaking at a women's retreat about an hour from her home, she arrived to find only one car parked near what looked like the major entrance. As she parked next to it, she saw an adorable, bright, bubbly blond opening her trunk. Marita went over, introduced herself, and asked this Sanguine if she knew where they should go. Neither one had any idea, but they just decided to unload their cars and march toward the big door. Fortunately, it was unlocked.

By the time the two of them had unpacked their products and set up their booths, they were best friends. At the end of the day, Marita and this new best friend, whose name she can no longer remember, were pledged to each other forever. They exchanged business cards and really meant to keep in touch.

When Marita arrived home, Chuck asked, "How was your day?" He wasn't looking for a detailed account of the entire day, but when you ask Sanguines how their day went, you get the whole story. She was explaining her new best friend when Chuck interrupted. "Marita, you cannot make new best friends every day."

"Why not?"

"Relationships take time to build. If you have one or two best friends in a lifetime, that's all you can expect."

"That's all in a lifetime? What a depressing thought!"

Only Sanguines gather up new best friends like picking daisies. "We just clicked," is what they say. They don't need to know who you are, what you do, or where you live, as long as you click. This tendency can cause conflict in a marriage like Marita and Chuck's, where the husband and wife have such differing views on friendship. So if you are married to a Sanguine, try to remember that their tendency to make and drop friends is natural and unproblematic to them. Try to share their excitement about the new people and new experiences they encounter.

(Dis)Organized Fun

The word "fun" is the operative word for Sanguines. Even a little Sanguine child will ask, "Will this be fun?" The Sanguine sees fun as exciting, spontaneous, circumstantial, unplanned, spirit-led, surprising, adventurous, glamorous, unrestricted activity.

Sanguines don't want to be reminded of how much a trip is costing or reprimanded for eating two desserts. They want to stay up late and sleep until noon if they feel like it. If there are rules, criticism, or unexplained expectations, they pout and say, "This is no fun."

This tendency for unplanned fun can sometimes frustrate an organized Melancholy who has no innate need for this type of fun. To Melancholies, life is serious and to make trips successful, they must be planned way ahead. My husband, Fred, loves planning. He gets brochures, reads travel magazines, and asks other Melancholies what they enjoyed. He joins travel clubs that give discounts and buys time-shares that make our hotel stay appear free. He tracks our nine million miles on American Airlines, and if they fail to give us our mileage credit for each flight, he's on the phone to a supervisor.

But as a Sanguine, this organized fun used to annoy me. "Why can't we just go and see what happens?" I would say. All the planning and attention to details seemed to get in the way of my having a good time.

But now I have come to appreciate Fred's way of thinking because I recognize the benefits of planning ahead. I like the upgrades on airlines and the hotel suites for the price of a simple room. And all because Fred keeps records and plans ahead. I don't get involved in the Melancholy details, and then I'm surprised when I get there and see the Sanguine benefits that we would never have if I were in charge of our organized fun. I've finally learned that some adventures are more fun and exciting when the details are worked out ahead of time.

If you're married to a Sanguine spouse, you will have to remember their need for spontaneous fun. They may frequently surprise you with crazy ideas and try to talk you into joining their adventure. Although you may feel more comfortable with organized activities, it's important for you to give in to your Sanguine's need for excitement from time to time. Their lively spirit is sure to lead you into many memorable experiences together!

Married to a White Rabbit

Do you remember the White Rabbit in Alice's Wonderland? Scurrying frantically from place to place, he was always excusing himself with "I'm late! I'm late, for a very important date!" Some spouses are easily discouraged when they find themselves married to a Sanguine "White Rabbit" someone who can never get *anywhere* on time.

The Problem

Sanguine Josie was bouncy, bubbly, and loved to talk to people on the phone. Josie had a heart for helping hurting women and was one of the best pastoral counselors at her church, spending hours on the phone at a time. She blamed the burned broccoli and the missed meetings on the calls that came for help.

Her deeply sensitive and Melancholy husband, Mark, understood the need for Josie to use her counseling gift, but he found himself angry and resentful at his wife. He was never very upset by the missing dinners   those he could take care of himself. It was her tendency to run twenty or thirty minutes late for every meeting that got on his nerves. He considered it rude to keep people waiting and was frequently embarrassed by their tardiness.

Mark shared with me that friends would often hold dinners in the oven because he and Josie were late. Other times, they would cause a group of friends to miss the first part of a show. Sometimes Josie would come home late, and the kids would wait alone for hours after school. Nearly every time, Josie was late because she was taking one more call or talking through one more issue. When she finally hung up, she was slowed down by a makeup drawer and closet that were so unorganized it took more time to get ready than she expected. Often Josie would laugh the whole situation off and think it was funny that Mark got upset.

As he explained the problem to me, Mark paused and then sighed. "I feel bad that whenever she is late, I start to get super critical of all her faults. I know it only makes matters worse. But if she would just spend half the time she spends on the phone in organizing her life, we wouldn't have to be late for everything!"

The Solution

Mark was right. Josie needed to spend less time on the phone and more time on her obligations to friends and family. But Mark needed to change his response too. When Mark learned about the personalities, he softened toward his wife's talkative tendencies, learning that her ability to communicate and cheer people up was a blessing. He understood, though, that natural traits were not an excuse for going to extremes. He decided to change the way he responded to Josie.

The next week, when his boss invited them to dinner, Mark forewarned Josie that if she couldn't respect his need to be on time and give their hosts the same courtesy, he would drive his own car and she would have to drive separately. She laughed in disbelief and ignored him. That night, just as she was taking the curlers out of her hair, the phone rang. Mark looked at Josie as they exchanged silent but clear communication. Josie took the phone anyway, smiling. "Oh, honey, I will just be a minute, I promise!" When Josie finally hung up forty minutes later, Mark was gone.

At first Josie was shocked and hurt. Then she became angry. "I drove like a bat out of you-know-where," she recalls. And when she arrived, she marched right up to Mark, ready to burst with anger!

Mark gently took his wife by the arm and walked out to the patio. He explained to her, "Josie, sweetheart, I love you. I hated driving away without you as much as you hated me doing it. I know that those people from church who call you need you. But *I* need you too. I need you to honor *my* emotional needs. I'm your husband. Being prompt is very, very important to me. I don't feel that you love me when you are always late. Won't you please stop and listen and understand that?"

Josie felt terrible. Mark was right. He put up with a lot from her, and she had been very self-righteous. She was more interested in the people who called on the telephone than she was in her own husband. Josie started thinking about her actions and realized that part of the reason she acted as she did was because she didn't want anyone telling her what to do. She laughed at herself when she realized that she had been acting like her six-year-old daughter! And she vowed to start acting more like a courteous adult.

Sanguines, ever childlike, sometimes struggle with schedules, having to do what others expect, or just being quiet when someone is trying to complete their own project. Like Alice's rabbit, Sanguines can stay lost in childhood patterns, unable to find their way back to the real world. Mates married to Sanguines can best communicate their needs, not by being critical, but by showing the Sanguine that respect for their needs is how they feel loved.

Sanguines *always* understand the need for love.

Poor Baby

Sanguines need lots of affection and approval, especially when they are sharing their troubles. A Melancholy spouse may want to analyze the problem, a Choleric will surely try to solve it, and the Phlegmatic is likely to nod and listen without hearing a word. But what Sanguines really need at the down times is a hug and someone to feel sorry for them.

When Marita comes home from a trip in which all kinds of funny-bad things have happened, she wants to entertain her husband, Chuck, with all her follies. Because of his Melancholy nature, he wants to stop her story, ask her how she could have done such a dangerous thing, and tell her not ever to do that again. But these lessons slow down the momentum of the story, and sometimes end it completely. Marita does not appreciate Chuck's wisdom when she's simply trying to share her struggles. "All I want is sympathy, not instruction," she told me.

In order to solve this problem, they have come up with words that let him know if this is just one of her adventure stories or a serious problem. She calls the first type her "Poor Baby" narratives. When she is going to tell him a pitiful story about her horrendous day, she starts by saying, "This is a 'Poor Baby.' I want to tell you what happened, but I don't want you to try and fix it. Just hug me and say, 'Poor Baby. Poor Baby.'"

When she really has a problem she'll say, "I need a therapist. Help me."

Chuck is a therapist and has good advice that Marita can truly appreciate when she has asked for it. He is relieved that she now gives clear signals, and he says, "It's much easier now that I don't have to be a mind reader!"

Make sure you offer your Sanguine mate plenty of "Poor Babies" when they share their struggles with you. It may be tempting to solve everything for them or scold them for their errors, but this is sure to make their day worse. Instead, let them have your sympathy, and in no time they'll be showing their Sanguine smiles.

I Ran into the Police Car!

Sanguines are constantly looking for adventure and fun. But sometimes their eagerness for spontaneous activities causes them to act without thinking, causing frequent mishaps. Spouses of a Sanguine will have to become adjusted to their mate's accident-prone nature and learn to handle mishaps with grace.

Sanguine/Choleric Connie says that one of the great things about being married to a Phlegmatic man is that he never screams, rants, or raves when she has crazy mishaps. He just gives a quiet, "I would have expected that. I'll take care of it for you. That was not a very smart thing to do."

One day Connie backed her car into a parked police car that had its red lights flashing and whirling on the roof. Can you imagine her husband's response if he were Choleric? "You what! Couldn't you see the lights? Are you blind? That is the stupidest thing you've ever done! What do you want me to do about it?"

Connie called her husband to report her tragedy. "I ran into the police car!"

Gene didn't get upset; he just asked, "Was the policeman nice to you? Are you all right? I'll be right down."

Your Sanguine spouse may drive you crazy with their frequent accidents. But unless you want to develop high blood pressure, you will have to learn to accept that their propensity to get into trouble is a part of their personality. You may want to give them lessons that can prevent future mishaps, but always remember to affirm them by telling them that you love them and want them to be safe.

Instant Wallpaper

Sanguines often tend to underestimate the amount of time it will take them to complete a project. They are often scurrying to finish their projects at the last minute and cutting corners to get it done in time. This can be an especially bothersome habit in a Sanguine with Choleric tendencies. Their Choleric drive to start new projects combines with their overly optimistic Sanguine nature to create sloppy and rushed projects.

Sanguine Sharon loves spontaneous plans, last minute chaos, frenzied thinking, and messes that turn into memories! She enjoys birthing a grand idea and then scrambling to finish her creation in the same afternoon. Since it's more fun to hurry on to the finish, she doesn't mind cutting corners or hiding messes in cabinets, closets, and drawers. She's open enough to tell everybody who will listen that her dinner dishes are hiding in the oven from last night and that her clothes have been in the washer for three days because she's had too many chaotic disasters happen.

Her husband, Dale, by contrast, loves plans, organized schedules, and perfect harmony. He would prefer not to see messes, and he does not believe in cutting corners for any reason. Of course, if he ever did need to hurry through a project, he wouldn't go telling everybody about it like Sharon does!

Years ago, before they understood personality differences, these differences made their married life hard. Sharon would drive Dale crazy with her frequent and hurried projects. None of them were up to his perfect Melancholy standards.

One day Sharon invited some old friends for dinner. She wanted to make a grand impression, so when the day arrived, she flew to the grocery store and bought a crown pork roast with all the trimmings. She cooked from early morning until noon, making everything from scratch, including dressing, pies, and cakes. At noon she suddenly had the grand idea that it would be really impressive if her dining room was wallpapered and the curtains were up.

She quickly calculated that if the kids cleaned up the other rooms and Dale helped set the table at the appointed moment, everything would be ready at 6:30. To her, the plan seemed flawless. But then Dale came home.

When Dale came home to find her hanging wallpaper, he was not happy. He couldn't believe that she thought she could hang paper in one afternoon. Anyone who had a mind would know that a perfect wallpaper job takes many tedious hours. He examined her edges and corners and said, "I can't believe you have done this to our dining room!" Sanguine Sharon was shocked with his disfavor. It had been an exciting project until he came home!

By that point the kids were running through the house, jumping over couches, and screaming with delight that company was coming and they were going to have a real meal. Dale became more and more agitated, while Sharon finished the wallpaper, hung the temporary curtains, and ran to dress the kids in their coordinating outfits. Soon she was agitated too, wishing that Dale would help her get everything ready.

When they broke into arguing as the clock approached 6:15, she asked him, "Could you just pretend not to be mad at me so we can make the most of the last fifteen minutes before they come?"

The dinner ended up being a huge success, and the house looked beautiful. The kids used their manners, they looked perfect, the food turned out great, and the wallpaper didn't fall off the wall. And Dale gained his composure after their guests walked in the door.

Since this experience so many years ago, Sharon and Dale have both learned about the personalities. Over time, they have become more accepting of each other's personality traits. Sharon has learned to slow down and be more precise in her work, to plan and not respond to every impulsive urge. And as a result, she doesn't drive Dale crazy anymore.

Dale still laughs when she gets herself in trouble, but now he's used to Sharon's last minute projects and isn't as shocked as he used to be. Understanding their personality differences has helped them to grow up and grow closer.

Shoes in View

Because Sanguines so frequently start on last minute projects, they inevitably end up requesting help. With their charming and childlike ways, they can often talk anyone into finishing a project for them. If you're married to a Sanguine, don't be surprised if you often find yourself finishing or fixing their projects.

When Sanguine combines with Choleric in a personality, this person will be especially sly about getting others to do their work for them. The Choleric side of the personality develops a plan and recognizes every opportunity to control a situation. And the Sanguine charm makes others oblivious to their plot and willing to help because the Sanguine looks so helpless. Unfortunately, the Sanguine/Choleric also dislikes details and rarely has a project well planned out. In the end, they usually get what they want, but someone else does all the real planning and working for them.

Carol moves with the decisive pace of the Choleric and the wide-eyed innocence of the Sanguine. She gives the impression of Lucille Ball, hands up, eyes fluttering. Men she doesn't even know open doors for her in supermarkets   they are certain she wouldn't find her way out without them. She has this hopeless look down to an art form, and everyone seems to respond to the "Lucy" in Carol.

What most don't see is that the Choleric in Carol is able to take charge of anything or anybody. She doesn't have to be asked, she only has to sense the incompetence of others, and she will seize control. She is very aware of her Sanguine/Choleric personality, and she has fun making her life fit whatever situation arises. "Give me anything but boredom!" she exclaims.

As with many Sanguines, Carol loves shoes, and she likes being able to see them all in a glance. One day she found a large, bright-red shoe bag that hung over the back of a door and held twenty pairs of shoes. Buying this solved her shoe problems, and she filled it up with shoes and hung it on the back of the bedroom door. Filled to its capacity, this bag took up so much space that you could only open the door half way.

"What is this?" her husband, Gordon, asked.

"My new shoe bag. I've gotten my shoes all organized by colors," Carol answered.

"But you can't get into the room," Gordon said in a depressed tone.

"Of course you can. You just walk in sideways."

Gordon pretended to ignore the problem—as he did all problems—but each night he would push the door against the wall and pretend to slither painfully through the space. Carol ignored his actions. "Actually it was the most physical thing he'd done all day. I rather enjoyed it."

When his soft nightly groaning didn't bother Carol, he tried measures desperate for his Phlegmatic nature. "You have got to get these shoes out of the bedroom," he said with a long-suffering-husband sigh.

Quickly seizing an opportunity to buy something new, she said, "That's fine. I'll go buy some shelves for the closet." She wasn't sure where she'd fit any in, but it was worth a try. She grabbed her jacket and in true Sanguine fashion was quite excited about going to the store.

"Where are you going?" Gordon asked.

"Out to buy shelves," she replied in her helpless and charming way. She'd seen some shiny white ones at Home Depot that anyone could put together in a minute.

But for a change, her fluttering eyes didn't have the desired effect.

"You don't need to go to the store and spend money. We have bricks and boards in the garage. You can build yourself some shelves."

"Build shelves?" Suddenly what had started as an adventure had turned into plain work.

Not wanting to be defeated, she went to the garage and found boards of assorted sizes. She didn't have a yardstick handy so she ran upstairs and walked it off by her feet. Six full feet plus one without toes. She rushed down before she forgot.

Unfortunately, she had to back out one car to make room for the boards on the floor. She could see she couldn't saw them on the floor, so she propped the boards against Gordon's car and plugged in the chain saw. This noise alerted Gordon to potential tragedy, and he came out to see what she was doing. He shut the motor off and asked, "Did you measure the space?"

"Oh yes," she said proudly. "Six regular feet and one with no toes." Gordon raised both eyebrows at once.

He left in disgust, measured the closet, and cut the boards accurately, making rounded corners so they'd fit better. He carried the boards to the bedroom and left her to bring up the bricks until she dropped an armload, gouging a hole in the wall. Then he carried the rest up with a few heavy sighs and went back to his TV in hopes of receding from the troubles of this stressful afternoon.

Carol did her best to build those shelves on the bottom of a closet already overladen with long skirts, pants, and dresses. She put all her shoes on the shelves, but when she backed up to look at her work, she couldn't see her shoes because the clothes covered the shelves. So the next day she took the shoes out and arranged them under the bed behind the dust ruffle. All the heels were under Gordon's side, the dressy metallic flats across the bottom of the bed, and the work type along her side.

This new arrangement works well for Carol. She just picks up the dust ruffle on any side and there's a shoe in view. The shelves just sit empty in her closet   a reminder for Sanguine Carol that planning ahead could have saved her and her husband a lot of time and effort.

The Dead Sea and the Babbling Brook

Your Sanguine spouse is sure to keep you entertained throughout your life together. This energetic personality will always be open to adventure and loves spending time with others. But if you are a quieter personality, constant Sanguine chatter and activity will make you want to quiet down your spouse.

Betsy is a Choleric professional ventriloquist. She says it fits her personality perfectly. She can do a one-hour presentation and deliver all the lines herself. She is also in charge of all the puppets, and they can't say a word without her permission. "It's a lot easier than working with real people!" she says.

Betsy's Phlegmatic husband, Rod, is a physician at the Loma Linda Hospital. Betsy is a Certified Personality Trainer and does the children's story each week in her church, using her puppets to teach a life-changing principle.

When Betsy first met Rod, she fell in love with a "quiet, still waters" kind of man, and Rod fell in love with a cute "little bubbly brook who just babbled through life" kind of woman.

But after they had married for a few months, something began to happen to the beautiful scenery they had created together. Rod was starting to look more like the Dead Sea because he didn't move, and Betsy was looking more like a dreadful, dripping form of Chinese water torture because she wouldn't stop pressing Rod to move—*now!!!*

What happened? Well, Betsy now sees that Rod was expecting her to turn into the "quiet, still waters" that he was, and she was expecting Rod to turn into a "rapid, rushing river" who pulled everyone else along with its flow. Betsy even came alongside the "Dead Sea" and tried to dig trenches to get the water flowing, but all that happened is that she got stuck in the mud. And Rod came alongside Betsy and tried to quiet her down by putting rocks in her "babbling brook," but all that happened is that she got all dammed up.

Water is a very powerful force, and when used constructively, can be life-giving and a great source of energy. But when misdirected, it can erode any object it comes in contact with. This can happen rapidly or over a long period of time, but the result is always the same—it will wear down and eat away the foundation it comes up against.

In looking back at the beginning of their marriage, Rod and Betsy see that although they were always committed to each other, they had water damage from not allowing each other to be the water God created them to be.

Their story has a happy ending, though. Rod and Betsy learned about the four personalities, and now they understand each other's emotional needs and personalities and allow and encourage each other to be who God wants them to be. They did some major "environmental restoration." Now Betsy enjoys the quiet, still waters in her life, and Rod doesn't mind the bubbly brook that babbles through his life.

Like Betsy and Rod, other marriages with a Sanguine spouse are sure to have a "bubbly brook" flowing through the household. Your Sanguine spouse will fill your home with lots of laughter, love, and friends. You will often appreciate your Sanguine's friendliness, optimism, and cheerful attitude. And as you help them control their weaknesses, never forget to fill their emotional needs for affection, attention, and approval. No matter the mishaps or accidents you find them in, never forget that God gave you this sunny Sanguine spouse for a special reason.

five

THE MELODY OF THE MELANCHOLY

Nobody Knows the Trouble I've Seen

When Joan and her husband, Frank, first got married, he decided to give her dishwasher lessons. All the plates and bowls must be facing the same direction. No friendly ones looking at each other. All spoons were to go in one section of the basket, forks in another. Frank was determined to have all things done decently and in order. Joan thought this was a trivial problem and gave the authority of the dishwasher over to him. Like everything else in Frank's neatly organized world, he enjoyed loading the dishwasher "correctly."

Does Frank sound like a copy of your spouse? If you've found yourself with a person who has a place for everything and spends hours on tiny details, you are probably married to a Melancholy.

Melancholies are quiet and undemanding. They are creative and deep thinkers, and they like to be left alone. Melancholies also keep detailed schedules and respond well to an organized environment. They are always analyzing, ever reliable, and usually serious.

Melancholies like people who share their taste for intellectual and serious pursuits. They enjoy being with people who carry on sensible conversations and who do not try to lighten the mood with superficial banter. As a very thoughtful person, Melancholies are sensitive to the feelings of their family and friends.

People who are forgetful, late, or disorganized will quickly get on the nerves of a Melancholy. They do not like to be around unpredictable people and consider less intelligent personalities to be "lightweights."

If you are married to a Melancholy, you will enjoy reading this chapter and learning how to see the world from your spouse's perspective. Understanding this thoughtful personality will give you the key to filling their deepest needs.

Melancholy Emotional Needs

The Melancholy needs are based on inner emotions. Their heart's cry is "Support me, and don't make fun of me. Give me some space and silence."

The Melancholy's basic desire is to have everything done perfectly and in order. For them, there is no other way. When you do things late, sloppy, or not at all, they feel like you don't love them because if you did, you would make a great effort to do things right.

The following list will help you understand and meet the Melancholy emotional needs:

1. **Support:** They need to know you are "with them." They get easily hurt if you make fun of them or make them the butt of your stories. Don't ask, "What's the matter with you?" Instead say, "I can tell you're hurt, and I'll just sit here until you feel like telling me."
2. **Space:** In contrast to Sanguines, Melancholies need their own space. They want to know that what is laid down on

the desk today will still be there tomorrow. They get depressed if their things are borrowed, ransacked, or ruined. Picking up a sticky pencil can send them to bed with a headache. Try to see that Melancholies have their own space and don't touch their things.

3. **Silence:** Realize Melancholies don't need noise, chatter, company, or chaos. They need a place where they can go to get away from the family. Respect their desire for silence and don't rush them from one social event to another.

4. **Stability:** Melancholies need to feel a sense of order in their lives. Try to respect their daily routines and only interrupt this pattern when you have a true emergency. When possible, help your Melancholy spouse keep to their schedule   this will save them from a lot of stress.

If you are a Melancholy, it's important to realize that no person can perfectly fill these needs. Life is not always perfect, and it's not always your spouse's fault when your schedule or personal space is disrupted. Sometimes time or circumstances may not permit your spouse to complete a project just the way you want it, but this does not mean that they don't love you. Always remember that we live in an imperfect world, and even you cannot always live up to perfect expectations.

Incarnation Celebration

Melancholies take life seriously and have no tolerance for frivolity. All things have purpose and order, and there is little time to waste on unproductive activities. They feel most Sanguines are lightweights and can't understand why so many people seem to be taken in by them. After all, Sanguines rarely do things to Melancholy perfection.

A friend of mine attended a church that had a Sanguine pastor for many years. Every Sunday was an exciting event. Pastor Popular was such fun that all the children loved him and related to him as a large-sized child. He thought up fun things to do in church and once a month he put on a "Happy Birthday Jesus" party. Every child who had a birthday that month could come up front at children's sermon time, and the whole congregation would sing to them. The pastor would tell a warm fuzzy story from Jesus' childhood, give them a chocolate bar, and send them back to their seats. The monthly event was such a hit that families from the community would come on their child's birthday.

When Pastor Popular was called on to a bigger church, he was replaced by a highly educated Melancholy. Pastor Perfect felt ill at ease with parties   especially those held during the church service. When he tried to cancel the "Happy Birthday Jesus" party, parents complained. "That's the best attendance we get all month!"

Yielding to pressure, the Melancholy pastor renamed the popular "Happy Birthday Jesus" party the "Incarnation Celebration." He gave a theological message, presented "Jesus Saves" buttons, and stopped passing out those sticky candy bars. Attendance dwindled, and many children didn't care to go up front for a "dumb" button. Of course, the Melancholies were pleased with the new pastor's depth. But everyone else missed the fun. One Sanguine mother was even heard to say to her husband, "If they're going to call this 'Carnation Celebration,' why don't they at least give each one of us a carnation!"

The "Incarnation Celebration" had a short life. Soon, the children were just shuffled off to Junior Church.

Melancholies are the first to suggest that the fun has gone too far, and it's easy for their thoughtful sensibilities to be offended by the fun activities of those around them. Many spouses respond to this Melancholy restraint like the parents in this story, with verbal complaints and ridicule. But their negative comments are likely to hurt the sensitive Melancholy.

Instead, try to focus on the positive aspects of this Melancholy trait. Rarely do Melancholies ruin a serious moment with ill humor. And their thoughtfulness prevents them from hurting others and makes them quick to notice when others are hurting. Give your Melancholy spouse respect and support in their serious endeavors, even as you encourage them to have a little fun.

Sock Bumps

Is it possible to have a marriage problem over folding socks? One day I used the socks as an example in speaking. Adorable Sanguine/Phlegmatic Linda came up to me and said, "I have the sock problem too."

Linda, like me, grew up rolling socks in balls. My brothers even created games with these sock rolls by throwing them from one end of the room into the wastebasket at the other end. When Linda married Melancholy Jim, one of her first lessons was how to fold socks correctly. He informed her that all the heel bumps must be facing in the same direction. She didn't even know what heel bumps were so he showed her how to fold the socks once and pile them with the bumps facing in the same direction.

She told me this story in wide-eyed disbelief that such a dumb thing mattered to anyone. "He even told me he couldn't sleep at night if he thought his bumps weren't headed in the same direction." Linda laughed and told me the rest of the story.

Linda met Jim while they were both working as internal auditors at an electric utility company. She was attracted to Jim's neatness, his control of his workspace, and his quiet dignity. When they discussed getting married, she thought he would be a stabilizing influence in her Sanguine life, and he appreciated her enthusiasm for having fun.

But the endearing qualities that attracted them soon turned into a battleground. In their home office, Linda would leave stacks of mail on the counter, files on the floor, and the drawers open so she could see what was in there. Jim would walk in and slam shut the drawers, asking her to keep her mess confined to her own workspace.

After Linda read *Personality Plus* she and Jim took the Personality Profile together. She found out she had some Sanguine in her but her years of auditing (such a boring job) had wiped any fun out of her life. She discovered that Melancholy Jim wasn't intentionally trying to irritate her. He needed the house to be in perfect order because it was part of his personality's needs. And she learned how to operate outside of her own personality comfort zone in order to meet her Melancholy husband's needs.

After learning the trademark of Melancholy perfection, she decided to give Jim a surprise Christmas present, a gift of love that took almost a year to complete. It was a gift that no amount of money could buy   an old-fashioned spring-cleaning to organize the entire house!

To set this plan in motion, she forced herself to clean fifteen minutes a day, four times a week. Even she could clean for fifteen minutes a day! The goal was to move from room to room, closet to closet, drawer to drawer, and all through the house in one year. She set a kitchen timer for fifteen minutes each day, so she wouldn't work too long. (It went against her Sanguine nature to work more than was necessary.)

In order to keep motivated, she created a reward system for herself to help her see progress. She bought a fluorescent orange sticker to put on her calendar for each day she spent at least fifteen minutes on cleaning. She called these chores her "trek through the treasure troves and trash." The orange stickers rewarded her, and each day as she put one up she would pretend the sticker said "Attagirl!"

By Thanksgiving Linda finally got around to the kitchen area, and in early December her goal was in sight! Somehow she had managed to keep "Jim's special Christmas gift of love" a complete surprise, even though he had noticed a difference in the house. He hadn't dared mention it for fear she'd quit.

On Christmas Day, she placed a cute card in the toe of Jim's stocking, telling him all the details of what she had accomplished. Then she led him around, opening drawers and closets displaying all of her hard work! Linda remembers, "From his grin, I could tell he was grateful for my gift of neatness and organization and was probably silently praying it would continue."

Keeping the house organized and the messy office in order brings joy to a highly Melancholy individual such as Jim, and Linda says it helps to motivate her daily to keep her desk a little neater than it used to be. After going to the home of a couple who is pleasant but messy, Linda says she has a new appreciation for Jim's approach to life. How about you? Perhaps you would like to spend not fifteen minutes, not one day, but one year of your life giving your Melancholy mate a gift of love.

Hopefully, Jim sleeps better at night knowing the house is in order and all his socks have their bumps facing in the same direction!

A Memorable Vacation

Another Melancholy characteristic is their close attention to details. A Melancholy is sure to keep their household in order, with every item perfectly in place. And their careful scrutiny of details can be a lifesaver when they are married to a scatterbrained spouse!

But to the spouse of a Melancholy, these perfectionistic habits can seem insane. To keep their marriage in balance, a Melancholy sometimes needs to forget about the details and simply enjoy a good time with their spouse.

Rhonda is a true-blue Sanguine married to Melancholy Rick. These two have radically different approaches to having fun. Being Melancholy, Rick likes order. He wants a goal to work toward, and he wants a strategy for reaching that goal. To Rhonda, this is the antithesis of the word "fun." She will admit that some planning is necessary   you don't pick up four kids for a vacation on the spur-of-the-moment. But she also believes a little spontaneity is necessary for a good time.

When they go to an amusement park, for example, Rick thinks the first order of business is to sit down, decide what each person wants to see, and formulate a plan of action. Rhonda is willing to plan out some of the big rides in order to avoid three-hour waits in line. But to her, any plan more elaborate than that borders on obsessive-compulsive.

On one occasion she and Rick took a trip to Florida without their kids and visited Universal Studios. The minute they stepped inside the park, Rick said, "Let's plan what we want to do today."

"Rick," she interrupted. "We're on VACATION. We left the kids behind. It's just you and me and the pavement. Let's do something really daring. Let's just go with no plan and see what happens."

Rick blinked. This was hard for his Melancholy mind to take in. Eventually, however, he surrendered. He tucked the souvenir map in his hip pocket, grabbed her hand, and started walking. A memorable vacation, to be sure!

Surf's Up and So Are Danders

Melancholies want everything in their life to look perfect, right down to the smallest detail. They dress in the latest styles, and their personal appearance is always neat, clean, and very proper. If they had things their way, they would have their spouse looking like a fashion plate too.

But since Melancholies often marry someone with a different personality, they find themselves frustrated with their spouse's less-than-perfect style. It's hard for them to understand why anyone would choose clothes or accessories that are eccentric or out

93

of step with the latest trend. If you are married to a Melancholy and you want to keep harmony in your marriage, it's important for you to express to them why you prefer your own style. And it's important for the Melancholy to realize their spouse's different preferences don't make them bad.

Melanie is a creative Melancholy whose attention to details served her well in her interior decorating career. One balmy summer evening, at the open house celebration of an ocean mansion she'd decorated, Melanie mingled with the crowd of local politicians, potential property owners, and a movie star or two. As she stood on the open balcony in pink peau de soie and polite conversation, she could not help but notice Roger. Roger was in real estate, tall, tan, and handsome, and ready with stories and jokes that kept the party going. Melanie was immediately drawn into the conversation by his charm, and later into his arms by his love. They were married a year later.

But like most marriages, the honeymoon period soon wore off, and Melanie found herself looking almost obsessively at Roger's faults. One of the things that bothered her the most was the way he dressed.

Roger grew up as a surfer in Southern California and still acted like a beach boy. Unless he had to attend a serious business meeting, he wore loud, garish Hawaiian shirts with colors that just didn't match anything. These shirts were a hobby for him, and he collected shirts from vintage clothing shops and searched for them on the Internet. The finishing touch was the way he let them hang over his pants in a way that Melanie just found tacky.

Melanie prided herself on looking stylish when they went out. As a Melancholy, she delighted in the beauty of texture, color, and design, and she took her personal appearance seriously. Roger loved Melanie's stylish appearance, but he wouldn't get rid of his shirts for her, no matter how hard she tried. "If he really loved me," Melanie thought, "don't you think he'd do what I ask? I admit I'm pretty bitter about it, but what can I do?"

Sanguine Roger just didn't want to part with those Hawaiian shirts. His Sanguine nature also took pleasure in color and design; he just expressed his artistic bent in a different way than Melanie. "My shirts are my artistic expression," Roger said. "Lots of people love to see which new pattern I've been able to find. The designs bring back nostalgic emotions to lots of people. Why can't Melanie see that? She's so darn picky!"

When Melanie and Roger read *Personality Plus* they both began to understand each other. Roger got smart and decided to describe how he felt about his shirts from an artist's viewpoint so that Melanie could better understand him. When Roger told her his shirts were like his artist's palette, and that he got as much pleasure from the fabrics and design as she did from her interior designing, her attitude changed.

Melanie realized that she was too worried about her own image and how people thought of her instead of caring enough about Roger's "bohemian" artwork. Sanguine Roger learned to develop some sensitivity to her. When they go out now, he asks her how important it is that he not wear Hawaiian shirts. If it really bothers her, he is willing to wear something else, just as long as she doesn't ask him to change every time. As a thoughtful Melancholy, Melanie values Roger's request for sincerity, and she has learned to let the Hawaiian shirts go for many occasions.

It may sometimes seem like a little thing is tearing the fabric of a marriage apart, but even the shirt you wear or don't wear can be part of God's design for your personality. Clothing yourself in understanding can make you truly a work of art!

Postnuptial Contracts

Melancholies require stability in order to enjoy life. So when their spouse frequently breaks promises or fails to perfectly live up to their deadlines or goals, Melancholies feel frustrated and unloved. Seeking assurance that things will be done perfectly,

Melancholies may demand promises that their spouse do things just as they say.

If you are the spouse of a Melancholy, you may feel offended or hurt when they make these demands. But try to see the situation from their perspective and you'll understand that this is their way of asking for support and stability. Your Melancholy spouse needs you to keep your promises, so don't make any that you do not intend to keep.

Andy loved Wendy's carefree touch because it complimented his more meticulous Melancholy nature. After the wedding, though, what Andy first saw as carefree now looked chaotic. "Wendy's sweet and I love her dearly, but she leaves things lying around the house for months on end. She's not really a slob, but it takes her forever to pick things up and put them away. It drives me nuts!" Andy reported.

Wendy admitted her Sanguine charm couldn't always calm Andy down. "He gets angry the most when he sees the desk we share in our bedroom." Because they both use the computer, she tries to keep it as neat as he wants. But she has so many fun projects that it takes her a long time to get things organized and put away. Eventually it gets done, but he hates to see her piles sitting there for weeks at a time.

Andy and Wendy decided to budget for a large desk that would give them each enough room for all of their papers and books. On a Saturday shopping trip, they found a large custom desk that would extend along the entire bedroom wall. Andy was thrilled about all the drawers, cupboards, and cabinets it had, and Wendy thought the whitewashed oak was light, airy, and perfect for their desert home. The minute they agreed it was perfect, a worried Andy began to imagine the huge mess their bedroom would be while everything got transferred from the old desk to the new set. He decided to set a boundary for his wife.

"Wendy, I think we should get this desk, but . . ."

Wendy interrupted, "I know, I know, you don't trust me to keep it clean. I promise I will."

"Well, honey, you've made promises before. I'd like you to sign a contract that you'll have everything from the old desk off the floor, anything out of the closets or wherever else put away in two weeks . . . or the desk goes back to the store."

Wendy hesitated, thinking this was a little controlling. But she realized that she hadn't lived up to her past promises, and Andy was dealing with mistrust she'd caused. Andy and Wendy both understood the four personalities, and Wendy remembered that a neat workspace, especially in their bedroom, was a strong emotional need for her husband.

"Okay, honey! I agree," Wendy smiled. "Where do I sign?"

Two weeks later Wendy was at the mall with her friend Ronda and happened to look at her watch. "Oh no! I have to get home!" Wendy almost screamed in panic.

"What's wrong?" asked Ronda, afraid Wendy had some family emergency.

"I forgot!" Wendy replied. "Today is the last day on my contract. I have to rush home and get that desk organized. I haven't even started!"

Wendy did get home on time, and that night the job was finished, much to her husband's delight. Wendy wasn't offended by Andy's request for a written contract because she realized her own weaknesses had deprived her husband of something he needed from her . . . a commitment to her promises. Wendy loved Andy and saw the limit he set as a loving act of a compromise on his part. After all, two weeks was pretty generous for a Melancholy!

"I'll Polish Him Up"

"By the time Larry and I had been married seven years and two children had been added to our family, he was rarely home. The very character qualities I'd appreciated in him in the first place were now sources of irritation. Why did I ever think his manic drive and opinionated attitudes were charming?"

So wrote Melancholy Kathy about the beginning of her difficult marriage. Although she didn't know about the personalities at that time, she knew she had expected a perfect marriage. She had gone to the right schools, read the right pre-marriage books, and was ready to put it all together. She even knew how to dress in fashion, and all her shoes and costume jewelry coordinated perfectly. What could go wrong?

Since she did all those right Melancholy things and still wasn't happy, she figured it must be Larry's fault. Larry was a powerful Choleric, with a touch of Sanguine charm that had pulled Kathy into marriage. But right from the beginning of their marriage Kathy saw there were holes in Prince Charming's armor. As she looked him over she saw rust spots she hadn't noticed before. "I'll rub them out," she thought. "I'll polish him up!"

Kathy set out to remake Larry into the perfect husband. She quickly fell into the Melancholy weakness of nit-picking and pointed out every little fault she saw in him.

Larry was perplexed by her actions. Why couldn't she accept him as he was? Other women found him handsome and charming, so why couldn't Kathy see him that way?

As he thought this over, Larry realized he was a lot happier away from home. But the more he stayed away, the angrier Kathy was when he came home. Then she would try even harder to make him into a perfect husband and make life at home even worse for him. As this cycle continued, Larry just started to stay away more often.

One morning he announced that he was flying to San Jose for the day. Kathy, feeling lonely and rejected, cried out, "Take me with you! I'll get the kids ready. We'll have a nice family day." Larry remembers her looking pitiful as she begged.

"No, Kathy, you can't go. This is business. You wouldn't fit in, to say nothing of the kids."

"If we can't go, why don't you stay home just once!"

Larry turned toward Kathy and said in a patronizing tone, "I'm doing this for you. I work all these hours to secure your financial future."

As Larry walked toward the car, Kathy yelled after him. "Money isn't helping me cope with these kids."

Larry called back, "Kathy, that's just typical motherhood blues. You'll be fine. I'll be home at ten tonight. You stay home and have a nice, quiet day with the kids."

"Quiet day?" Kathy screamed as Larry smiled and waved.

Kathy was furious as she hurled the half-eaten apple in her hand across the hall. The children watched in fright as the apple hit the wall and shattered. Apple pieces stuck to the ceiling and some dropped on the children.

Kathy ran to the bedroom, threw herself to the floor beside the bed, and began sobbing to God.

"Lord, make that plane crash! I don't care if he ever comes home again."

How did this attractive, intelligent Christian couple get in this kind of trouble? If we were taking this case to Ann Landers, we would get a clear and simple answer. He has to take her with him twice a month, and she has to realize the man has to go out and make a living, so she should encourage him and not be so selfish. But will this change their attitudes? They both knew what they should do, but neither one was doing it.

Larry looks back on this time in regret. "Kathy was no fun to be with. When I was home, she complained all the time. I couldn't fight it, so I learned to tune her out and watch TV." During that time, Larry didn't care to talk with Kathy because nothing he said could meet her perfect expectations. He tried to explain that the life-and-death stress of his job gave him a need for some peace and quiet at home. But sensitive Melancholy Kathy wanted some support and love. When he sat down quietly in his chair, she was there asking, "Why don't you talk to me anymore?"

Both Kathy and Larry pulled back and tried to live a phony peaceful life for the sake of the kids. Neither one wanted a divorce, but neither one was having their needs filled by their marriage. Life was out of control and no fun for Choleric/Sanguine Larry and totally out of order and imperfect for Melancholy Kathy.

Both of them prayed separately for restoration and understanding. Friends gave them books and tapes and tried to encourage them. Among the books was *Personality Plus*. Kathy read it, and they began to talk about their differences. This was the first meaningful discussion they'd had in months, and they began to see themselves in a new light.

Melancholy Kathy learned to appreciate the strength and charm of Larry's personality. "Different" had always meant "wrong" to her in the past. And as a perfect Melancholy, she had been very determined to change Larry's "different" personality because it wasn't perfect in her eyes. Learning the four personalities helped this Melancholy see that both of them could be right, even though they were different.

As Kathy began incorporating these ideas into relating to Larry, she didn't seem as unrealistic in her expectations of him. When she stopped making him feel like a failure and started giving him support, he was attracted to her again. His trips away from home became less frequent. And twenty-three years later, this couple's marriage has grown into an example they can share together at marriage seminars.

Kathy's decision to love Larry, even though he didn't perfectly meet her expectations, provides an important lesson for all Melancholies. The urge to "polish up" your spouse may be strong, but remember that their different personality does not make them wrong. In fact, when you learn to appreciate different perspectives, you may just want to focus your polishing efforts on yourself!

Drapes and Window Swags

Can you create marriage problems by draping a bright fabric swag over a pole at the top of a large picture window? Columnist Michelle Slatalla says she did.

She came home one day to find her husband tearing down her dramatic swag, destroying the fabric and pole beyond repair.

Although she doesn't label her personality, she is an obvious Sanguine who thought draping material over the pole would be just the decorative touch the room needed. Her husband, a Melancholy, felt hurt that she hadn't asked his opinion. He tolerated the garish fabric as long as he could and then one day yanked it from its precarious holdings.

Michelle cried and wondered, "How could I have married a man who would make a drape assumption?" Her husband was confused by this response; he didn't realize he had married a woman who sobbed over swags!

Now that she has learned a few things about marriage, she looks back on the situation with understanding. "I wish I knew then what I know now. Instead of assuming that the wedding was a terrible mistake, and that we would have to return all those silver-plated cake plates, we could have addressed the real problem: our different expectations about marriage."

Different expectations for sure!

Melancholies assume that every project will be done perfectly, and they expect their mate to agree that anything worth doing is worth doing right. But the other personalities don't share the Melancholy desire for perfection. Sanguine Michelle certainly didn't expect that her perfect husband's response to a bright window swag would be tearing it apart!

Michelle's marriage counselor told them "to recognize disparities and negotiate compromises acceptable to both." Excellent advice   but will the average unhappy couple know how to put these words into effect or even know what these words mean? Only when we understand the personalities do we have a simple tool at our fingertips that can help us rebuild a shaky foundation and even laugh as we are doing it.

Melancholy Blues

With their thoughtful and sensitive nature, Melancholies can be easily hurt. Always wanting life to be perfect, they are frequently let down by the reality of an imperfect world. If you're married to a Melancholy, it's important to recognize the things that will make your spouse feel sad. As you come to understand their personality, you can give them support as they experience the Melancholy blues.

Sanguine/Choleric Marita gave me an example of how she has learned to react positively to Melancholy Chuck. When he is upset over something and headed for a depression, she no longer does her automatic challenge to him: "Shape up! That's nothing! Put it behind you and move on!" Those Choleric comments hit his sensitive Melancholy spirit all wrong, and he clams up and won't talk.

Instead, Marita learned the personality principle and started to deal with him according to his personality and not her own. Now when she sees the black cloud approaching, she sits down and says softly, "I can tell there's something bothering you. When you feel like it, please tell me."

In contrast to Marita, Lucy's brilliant Choleric husband doesn't understand the Melancholy personality. Lucy had been put in the position of editor of some denominational magazines, and the volunteers who were supposed to do the work took the job casually. They missed deadlines, and they didn't seem to care. Melancholy Lucy wanted everything to be perfect and on time, but she found it difficult to reprimand these people.

One day when she'd been under stress, she wanted to talk to her husband, Doug, about her problems. She started to tell him about her difficulties with the volunteers and hoped to get some sympathetic support. As she looked up for an encouraging word, he gave her a typical answer. "It's simple. Just fire the whole bunch of them!"

Happy with his answer, he stood up and left the room as she moaned, "How can I fire them? They're volunteers."

Choleric Doug didn't respond very well to his wife's need for support. Had he paused to see things from her perspective, he would have realized that "just firing them" was an impossible solution for her sensitive and thoughtful personality. He should have simply offered a listening ear as she talked.

Always remember that Melancholies don't want to feel like you're waiting for them to "get over" their depression. They want somebody at their side to go through the down times with them.

Your Melancholy spouse will be a cherished friend in your lifetime together. Their meticulous attention to detail is sure to save your home and family from some disasters. And their sensitive nature will make them a thoughtful spouse and friend. Remember these wonderful traits as you help them avoid nit-picking and get them to have a little fun. No matter where you find yourselves together, offer your Melancholy plenty of space, silence, and support. God knew that this unique combination of traits was just the right person for you.

six

THE CLANG OF THE CHOLERIC

Seventy-six Trombones Take Charge

Anna is a hardworking mom who leads a prayer group called God's Garden of Prayer. After coming to one of my personality seminars, she informed me that I was being added to their list. She asked that I send her a monthly schedule so that she can pass this information on to her prayer group friends.

Now, I've had many well-meaning Christians say, "I'll pray for you." But Anna really does pray for me. For over fifteen years Anna and her prayer group have been holding me up in prayer. And each time when I arrive home from a ministry trip, I find a flowered card signed, "God's Garden is praying for you."

Anna's "get-the-job done" attitude is the mark of a true Choleric. This personality takes charge of any and every situation that comes their way. And their quick thinking gives them good judgment and makes them natural leaders.

Cholerics will get along well with people who are supportive and submissive. Anyone who sees things their way or lets them take credit for a project becomes a friends of the Choleric. But people who are lazy or just plain tired get on the nerves of Choleric powerhouses.

If these characteristics sound a lot like your spouse, you're probably marrried to a Choleric. It's important for you to understand this powerful personality so that you can learn how to meet their needs, respond to their controlling habits, and help them overcome their Choleric weaknesses.

Choleric Emotional Needs

In contrast to the Sanguine or Melancholy, the Choleric's needs are not "gimmes" or emotional. They are practical and simplistic. "Do what I say and do it now. MOVE!"

The Choleric's basic need is to be in control. Understanding this need alone is the key to understanding the behavior of your Choleric spouse. Sometimes a Choleric's tendency to take charge of all situations makes their spouse feel inadequate. It's easy to feel incompetent when a power-driven Choleric is in charge. But the Choleric desire for control has nothing to do with your level of ability at all. It's just that their personal security depends upon their controlling life   and you are a part of their life.

The following list will give you some advice on understanding and meeting the needs of your Choleric spouse.

1. **Appreciation:** Cholerics need to know that you appreciate all that they have done for you. And they have done much! Whatever is needed, they get it. And whatever is broken, they fix it. All they want from you is abundant thankfulness. "I can't believe you did all that!"
2. **Action:** Cholerics want action on your part. They love work and expect others to keep up the same hyper pace that they exhibit. They tend to marry Phlegmatics for their peaceful, nonconfrontational natures, but soon they get upset when

their mate needs a nap. "What's the matter with you! It's only 2:00 in the afternoon, and we've got the garage to clean!"

3. **Opportunity for leadership:** I raised my children in my Choleric personality. The motto was, "If mother stands, we all stand!" Cholerics cannot abide laziness, and they want to be leading the action. They expect you to rise, jump, run, work, and win all at their command. Make sure your Choleric spouse is given lots of opportunities to lead and don't challenge their authority in front of others.

4. **Something to control:** When you understand the Choleric personality, you realize they are not out to get you; that's just the way they are. They need something to control, and often they will start by trying to control their spouse. Offer your high-powered Choleric areas where they can be in control so that they don't feel the need to be in control of *you!*

If you are a high-powered Choleric, it's important for you to recognize how exhausting it can be for others to meet your emotional needs. Realize that three-fourths of the people you meet each day do not have your energy. And if you're not careful, your constant activity will scare them all off, and you may find yourself alone.

"That Was My Idea!"

Because Cholerics like to be in charge, they don't always respond well to other people's ideas. They want others to see them as the leader, and they don't like it when someone else has a better idea than their own. Often if they are given a little time, they will come to see the wisdom in someone else's idea. Then, watch out! There's no stopping them from the new project, which they will surely make their own.

Robert is a very powerful Choleric with few secondary traits. When he and his wife were going to sell their home, she suggested painting it so it would display more curbside appeal and possibly sell for a greater amount. His initial response was, "No, I'm not putting another cent into this house if we are just going to sell it." In typical Choleric fashion, he dismissed her idea and stuck to his own.

His wife, Sarah, just closed her lips and said a little prayer that he would come around. After a little while, Robert realized that painting the house probably was a good idea, and it wouldn't be too great a task. Just two days after his negative response, he got up early and headed to the store to purchase fifteen gallons of paint. The entire house was painted in one day with a little half-gallon airless sprayer. Sarah smiled, recognizing the strength of her Choleric mate   once he made up his mind, Robert would always go full force, 100 percent in the right direction.

Robert offers a clear example of what many Cholerics do in their marriage. He took no suggestions and refused to let Sarah win, even when he knew she was right. When he bought the paint and equipment, he knew it was because of her correct suggestion; he just couldn't give her the credit. Fortunately, Phlegmatic Sarah recognized his need to be in control and learned that it was best not to point out his inconsistencies. Even though it was her idea to paint the house, she knew it would be better to let Robert seize the project as his own. In her mind, she got the house painted and that was what she had wanted. After all, receiving praise doesn't paint a house!

If you have a Choleric spouse, it's important to keep their need for control in mind. When they refuse to acknowledge your good ideas, give them some time to think it over. And when they decide to do what you suggested, never say, "I told you so!" and expect their verbal praise. It's better to quietly smile as they carry out your project and accept that this is the Choleric way of letting you know they liked your idea after all.

Free Advice

As a person who thrives on power and control, Cholerics often tend to boss others around. They are so focused on being in charge that they don't realize they are bossy or give advice when it's not asked for. They just assume that if you are doing something wrong and they know a better way to do it, you would want to receive this information as quickly as possible. They dispense helpful information to any person in the midst of an erroneous act. "I'm sure you'd like to know a better way to do this."

Much to their amazement, not everyone appreciates their unsolicited advice. They have not learned that right isn't necessarily popular, and they just can't understand why people don't respond well to their advice. "If the dummies would only do it my way, we would all be happy."

Patty recently wrote to tell me about her own Choleric tendencies. She had never thought of herself as bossy and wondered why some defensive people didn't take kindly to her well-meant and accurate directions. "I feel the need to fix all of my friends' problems, straighten strangers' collars, and force my opinions on people when I feel passionately towards a certain topic."

Once, her local drugstore changed to a new phone system in order to free up wasted time for their employees. Patty would call regularly to check on film she would have developed, but she could no longer get through to a human. Never shy with her suggestions, she complained to the manager several times. "I don't want to talk to a machine. I want a real person. This new system isn't user-friendly!" She was surprised that he simply ignored her free advice. Instead, he would duck around the corner when he saw her coming.

On another occasion, she joined her mother and daughter for a Sunday lunch. They waited for twenty minutes to be seated when there were empty tables easily in sight. True to her Choleric nature, Patty asked to speak to the manager. He explained that they could only put a certain amount of people at each server's station. She immediately tried to tell him that it was ridiculous that so many people had to wait that long with all the empty tables available. He simply needed to hire more servers!

Patty's mother was embarrassed by her actions, and they didn't get a table any quicker. After thinking for a bit, she realized that the manager was probably aware of his problem, and she should have kept quiet.

On the bright side, Cholerics' tendency to speak up with their opinions is not limited to complaints. They are also the first to give compliments when a job is performed to their standards. As long as they feel like people have followed their lead, they are comfortable with letting them know they did a good job.

Your Choleric spouse may sometimes embarrass you with their tendency to give free advice to friends and family members. Try to remember that their efforts are well intentioned and instead of scowling at their advice, simply thank them for it and move on. You can also work to encourage them toward constructive uses of this tendency. Offer them lots of encouragement to get involved with activities where opinions and advice are needed.

Lazy and Crazy

Choleric spouses will always be busy with one activity or another. Less active spouses often look at this person and think they are crazy for attempting to accomplish dozens of tasks at once. But the Choleric spouse tends to look at other personalities as being lazy. They may have a tendency to nag or get upset with their spouse for not being more involved with their constant projects.

Sally came to our Personality Plus training workshop in order to learn how to teach these simple tools to others. A Choleric with some Melancholy traits, she wanted things done her way and done perfectly. She could accomplish more in a given day than some women could in a week. Even with six children to shepherd around town, she got them all delivered on time. She made them all matching plaid Sunday outfits, and people marveled at her ability to do everything quickly and well.

Sally's drive for perfection was fueled by the way she was raised. She grew up with parents who considered perfection as a norm, and she never felt she measured up. Before she learned about the four personalities, she had very low self-esteem and felt like she could never completely be what others wanted her to be.

As a powerfully driven Choleric, Sally often got upset with her Phlegmatic husband. The insecure Melancholy part of her kept her from complaining all the time, but what she saw as his laziness and indifference drove her crazy. Eventually, she had days when she couldn't take it another minute, and she'd explode. Her husband would listen quietly as she ranted on about their unfair relationship and her excessive burdens. "It's not right! I do all the work and you just lie around in that chair!" Of course, during those moments, Sally forgot that her husband worked six days a week to support his large family and that he needed his home and his chair as a haven of rest.

After learning about the four personalities, Sally began to appreciate the sweet, lovely, stable personality of the Phlegmatic. She knew she had lost sight of his strengths and of how his personality balanced her own. Once she saw that their differences weren't wrong, but were actually necessary for family harmony, her attitude changed and she became a more accepting wife. And without having to fear a nagging Choleric wife, her husband is smiling more and spending less time in his Phlegmatic chair!

If you're the spouse of a Choleric, you will often be amazed to see them juggle a crazy schedule. But remember that to the controlling and high-energy Choleric, this level of activity doesn't seem crazy at all. If you are a Choleric yourself, don't forget that most people don't share your drive and energy. Their need for some rest doesn't make them lazy   it only makes them human!

Airing Your Dirty Laundry

"Every strong-willed, bullheaded Choleric wife needs a loving husband to keep her balanced. Without Ed's peaceful nature, we would have been divorced long ago." This was the comment made by Choleric Marge as she explained how her Choleric tendency to nag has affected their marriage.

When Ed and Marge got married, Marge expected some household duties to be done without discussion. One of those duties was the proper placement of dirty laundry. They owned a clothes hamper, so Marge assumed that Ed would use it. At first she tried to be the dutiful wife and pick up his dirty clothes at the end of the bed, but that was short-lived. Soon her Choleric patience wore thin, and she offered him instruction on where to put his dirty clothes.

Phlegmatic Ed nodded in agreement and followed his wife's orders for a few days. And then there they were, on the floor again.

This time in a harsher tone, Marge warned him of the consequences of disposing dirty underwear on the floor: "If you expect these clothes to get clean, then put them in the clothes hamper."

Again Ed abided by her words for another couple of days, then went back to his old ways.

At this point, Marge gave her third and final warning: "If your clothes don't make it to the hamper, they won't make it to the washer!"

Ed never said a word; he just went into that sweet, stubborn, Phlegmatic mode. His dirty clothes pile grew and grew as Marge bit her lip in determination not to pick them up so she could teach him a lesson.

Finally that day arrived. Ed got out of the shower and started to dress, only to discover he had no clean underwear. He was furious. He ranted and raved as Marge stood smugly by. "I told you if you didn't put your clothes in the hamper, they wouldn't get washed," she reminded him. She took great satisfaction in the fact that her husband wore dirty underwear to work that day. She had won!

Or had she?

Not until she understood the personalities did Marge realize that her threats could win the battle but actually lose the war. In the case of their battle over the laundry, Marge had made her point, but she still didn't get Ed to pick up his clothes the way she wanted him to.

Knowledge of the personalities enabled Marge to understand the temperament of the Phlegmatic so that she could come alongside her husband and become his ally on the home front, instead of his nagging enemy.

Now if Ed drops his dirty laundry on the floor, she rarely makes a fuss. She tries to put herself in his shoes. And that helps her remember that sometimes it's worth letting a battle go so that they can both win the war.

A Marriage Made in Heaven

Cholerics' driven personalities make them great leaders. They are wonderful at motivating others and getting the job done. But this strength can turn into a weakness when it comes to marriage. Hard-nosed Cholerics don't want to take the time to understand their spouse's point of view. They just want to see things get done their way, since they assume it's the best way. As a result, they may find themselves controlling and stifling their mate's personality.

As with so many women, Cheri dreamed of the happily-ever-after life. She grew up in the South where women were expected to be demure, soft-spoken, and submissive. Cheri went to the right schools, came from the right family, and dressed in the right clothes. She played her role well and hid her Choleric nature from her family and friends. "Women don't give strong opinions," her mother always said.

When it was time for a proper girl to marry, Cheri won the prize. Randy was picture-perfect and had charm beyond anyone's expectations. His sense of humor, optimism, confidence, and personality were just what Cheri wanted. Everyone loved Randy, and nothing seemed to bother him. The older ladies in the church fawned over him, and the young ones wished he'd chosen them instead . The wedding was the society event of the year, complete with *Gone with the Wind* gowns and picture hats.

"A marriage made in heaven," the church ladies sighed.

But soon this heavenly marriage began to lead toward trouble. After six years, Cheri didn't know what had happened to the man she had married. He was no longer the one who took her out on dates just to talk, who had big dreams and was confident he would reach them, who made her laugh, and whom everyone liked. In his place was a man who couldn't make decisions, wouldn't share his thoughts and feelings, and who was no longer fun-filled but dread-filled every time they had to communicate. This was not the Prince Charming of her fairy-tale expectations.

What had happened to this fairy-tale marriage? When we understand the personalities we can realize why this couple had troubles. Cheri had spent her life as the sweet Southern princess, and her genteel ways hid her ability to control everyone in her life. After her wedding, she could hardly wait to polish up her new jewel. In true Choleric fashion, she believed he would be forever grateful! Randy had no idea there was anything that needed improvement. Everyone loved him! Even his mother-in-law thought he was precious. Why was his beautiful wife the only one who couldn't accept him the way he was?

Finally, Cheri reached a point when she got down on her knees and through tears cried out to God, "I know when I got married, I promised you it was for life, but I can't go on this way. I have done all I know how to do and nothing works. I'm willing to do whatever it takes to save my marriage. Please, do something!"

While she was still on her knees praying to the Lord, her phone rang. It was her friend Lynn, and Cheri began to pour out her heart. After she finished, Cheri was stunned to find out that Lynn had suspected their problems all along. Lynn recommended my book *After Every Wedding Comes a Marriage* and added, "You won't like it, but it's what your marriage needs."

As she read of God's plan for marriage, Cheri realized she had followed her own plan. She had not been using her personality to complement her husband but as a weapon to get her way. Even though she had married him for his pleasant Sanguine/Phlegmatic ways, she had tried to take control and turn him into something different. She had removed his confidence and not responded to his humor. And she had ridiculed him in front of others. Ignoring God's plan of submitting to Randy's leadership, Choleric Cheri had been using all her manipulative ways to control him.

It took a lot of hard work, some of it very painful, to restore Cheri and Randy's marriage. But when Cheri learned to accept Randy as he was and leave the changing to the Lord, the charming man she had married returned, and so did his beautiful wife. She now enjoys his humor, lingers in his conversations, and relaxes in his leadership, all because she went to the Master Builder and asked him to show her how to restore what she had unknowingly torn down.

Isaiah 58:11–12 says, "The LORD will guide you always; he will satisfy your needs." If you are a Choleric, these are especially important words to remember. Instead of trying hard to change your spouse into what you want, enjoy God's life-changing power in your own life. And instead of taking charge of every situation, learn to let God be your guide. Not only will this truth enrich your personal relationship with God but it will also help you deal with your marriage in a noncontrolling way.

Check the Calendar

Because Cholerics are so good at handling multiple tasks, they tend to have a detailed schedule that they can keep track of in their heads. Though a Melancholy may be able to master the details, Sanguines and Phlegmatics are quickly lost and find it difficult to remember so many different things at one time.

Cholerics, men or women, have an inner need to put down those who don't move fast enough or think like them. When pointing out faults doesn't work, the Cholerics make snide comments or direct insults. But when Cholerics put their powerful strengths to work, they can come up with solutions that don't make their spouse feel stupid.

Choleric Karen is married to a Phlegmatic who has a hard time tracking the details. She is fast and wants constant action—he moves at a slow pace and likes to be still. She thinks about the next project before she's finished with the current one   he's got all he can handle concentrating on the task at hand.

In the area of their differences, Karen put her Choleric strengths to good use, finding solutions that would not make her husband, George, feel stupid or hurt. One problem was in the area of scheduling. She had her schedule set for a year ahead, but he never seemed to know where she was going next.

"I was so frustrated about him not knowing our schedule," Karen shared with me. She would keep a detailed calendar with everything written down and a list of things to do by each event. Then she would tell him that they were scheduled for something and expect him to remember. But he would frequently forget, and it made her crazy! He tried personal calendars and computer programs, but these simply didn't suit his Phlegmatic nature. No matter what she tried, he couldn't stay up to date with her lists and plans.

One day she hung a monthly calendar on the wall next to where he shaved every morning. She put a list called "my plans and projects" along with their joint schedule on the calendar. He loves it! He can now look at it every morning and see what is coming up next week and next month. He is rarely unaware of their schedule, and they don't argue about it anymore. To Karen's delight, he now puts things on the calendar for her to see!

What a difference it can make in a marriage when you aim to meet your mate's needs instead of checking to see if you are getting your fair share. Life isn't fair and you may not get your share, but you'll be a lot happier in the process if you give graciously without looking for a return on your investment. When the Choleric puts their strengths to good use instead of using them to chide others, they will see a great return for the effort.

When the Pursuit Ends . . .

Many women married to Choleric men have told me that the pursuit was the exciting part of the dating relationship for these purpose-driven men. But their attitude quickly changes to, "Now that we're married, let's get down to business." There's little thought of the fluffy, fun, emotional needs of the wife. She interprets this Choleric businesslike attitude to mean "He doesn't love me anymore." He interprets her whining as immaturity. "Grow up. What have I got here? A child?"

Not only does the Choleric man see hurt feelings as immature, but he can't understand why his wife doesn't want instant answers to her problems. Men don't realize that women, especially Sanguine women, want to talk about the problem, not solve it. Fred once said to me in the middle of a dramatic tragedy I was reenacting, "I don't need to hear all the details. Is there a problem here that we need to solve?"

Shirley told me about how this problem cropped up in her own marriage. "At first I was attracted to his looks, admired his brains, his goals, and his independent nature," she shared. However, after marriage, his goals and independent ways became a big obstacle for her. She was a Sanguine who wanted to be dependent on him for everything. She wanted to have lots of fun, attention, and acceptance, but his goal-oriented lifestyle was not fun anymore.

Shirley's Choleric husband, however, wanted her to be independent and able to take charge of the family when he was traveling and working long hours. As a Choleric, the challenge had been in pursuing Shirley before marriage. But now that the pursuit was over, he had mentally moved on to other challenges with his work and with the family, and he didn't want to deal with the "gimme" needs of the Sanguine anymore. Since he stopped meeting her needs, Shirley felt that she no longer had to meet his needs either. These attitudes created great struggles and arguments during the years of raising their family.

Shirley's Choleric husband, as a military officer, was used to giving quick responses to constant conflicts. Day after day he was on alert, defending the country. When he came home to Shirley, he wanted to be helpful and solve her problems. If nasty women upset her, he offered a simple solution   just ignore them. But all she wanted was for him to listen to the humorous details and praise her for having lived through another day.

For those of you married to a Choleric, you will relate to Shirley's story. Try to remember that your spouse's responses aren't intended to hurt you. If they seem to be short and to the point, it is only because that is the way Cholerics operate. For those of you who are the impatient Choleric, learn to listen to your heart a little more often. Remember that for the other personalities, quickly solving a problem and then moving on makes them feel unimportant and uncared for. Instead, develop a compassionate heart and big ear for listening to your mate.

Fast and Furious Marries Slow and Steady

Cholerics often tend to marry their opposite personality, the Phlegmatic. This combination joins an extremely driven and constantly active personality with a very calm, inactive, and passive personality. God must have a sense of humor to pair up such odd couples.

But sometimes God's people fail to appreciate the patchwork of personalities he brings together in different combinations. In many Christian communities, women are expected to be humble homemakers who worship their strong dynamic spiritual husbands, who in turn dote on their wives. What a pretty picture! The men are all Choleric leaders, the women submissive Phlegmatics, and the children are Melancholies who study hard, memorize their verses, and sing in the junior choir. Sanguines don't fit in these churches because they are too loud and excitable and don't appear to have spiritual depth.

With this "ideal," what does the church do when a family arrives with a strong, controlling mother with uncontrollable children and a father who doesn't care? Do you send them to another church? Without an understanding of the four personalities, churches don't make the best use of powerful Choleric women, quiet gentlemen, or inquisitive children.

Karen and George represent this couple. She is the fast-paced female executive in a man's world. She travels around the world on business and is an applauded success. Phlegmatic George is equally adept in his business world and is not threatened by Karen's achievements. He is always at peace and has a much quieter personality than his Choleric wife.

Before knowing the personalities, Karen tried to push him into more activity and wondered when he was going to change and become more like her. She felt that he wouldn't be respected in the church unless he started showing his leadership ability. Karen tried to push, but he stayed firm.

With these differences, it would have been natural for them both to pull apart and go their separate ways, but they agreed to come in from their extremes and find a middle road. They have done this with love, a positive attitude, and a growing sense of humor. "One thing that saved us," Karen says, "is that both of us have some Sanguine in us, which allows us to laugh at our differences."

How have these two people stayed happily married for thirty-five years? Karen shared some of her practical answers with me:

1. "I've tried to become more like him by slowing down, resting, and being calm in a crisis. He has tried to become more like me by participating in my projects and works at showing excitement when I need him to."
2. "He has learned to get to parties and enjoy himself (which, by the way, is important to me because I don't have any fun if I can see or sense he is unhappy). I often thank him for going with me to an event, and he always smiles and says, 'I know you love a party!'"
3. "I have learned to stay home and enjoy a slow, easygoing day. I can put my agenda aside on a Saturday and take a ride in the country, even though it has no purpose at all. I admit that I like myself better since I have taken on some of his traits."

Karen and George have proven that a strong Choleric woman can live with a soft-spoken Phlegmatic man and both can be exemplary Christian leaders. They have both cared enough to read, study, take seminars, and discuss their differences. They respect each other's God-given personality strengths and have learned to overlook the weaknesses. They aren't what we think of as the typical church couple, but their Bible study group loves them, and they are proof that any combination of personalities can work to bring glory to God.

The Miraculous Ministry of "Shut Up!"

Religion is often a marriage problem with couples, even when neither one of them is particularly religious. Scoffing at one's denominational background can send a weak believer hustling off to church, just to make a point.

One of the Cholerics' wonderful personality traits it their dynamic commitment to faith. Once this personality makes a commitment to Christ, there is no stopping their works of Christian service and devotion. The drive and activity of a Choleric make them natural evangelists, wanting to turn everyone they meet into an instant believer.

Jaque and Chris were a Choleric/Phlegmatic combination who had experienced a great deal of conflict in their marriage. Everything from money to food became a topic of dispute in their troubled relationship. Unfortunately, they didn't have a shared faith to bring them together, but instead found themselves butting heads over religious issues as well. At several points in their marriage, they had considered divorce because they just did not seem cut out for each other.

When they had first gotten married, they never talked about religion. But it came to be an underlying problem for them. Chris was raised Catholic and believed that was enough to get him to heaven. Jaque was a late bloomer to the faith, but when she came to believe, she believed hard. Chris certainly didn't want her trying to change anything about him or telling him he needed a personal relationship with Christ when he'd been a faithful altar boy for years. But, of course, Jaque was tenacious and was going to lead him to the Lord one way or another.

At one point, this conflicted couple began attending Bible classes together. As part of the class, they journaled each day. Their journals took on the form of a personal dialogue with God, and through their journals they began to hear what each of them needed to hear. They finally quit praying for a "better marriage" and asked instead to see the glory of the Lord in their marriage.

Jaque began to realize that her Choleric sermonizing was building a bigger barrier than a bridge to faith for Chris. As she once shared with me, "When I finally sought the Lord for help, he lovingly but firmly began to show me that I was the problem and needed to attend to my own relationship with God."

As Jaque submitted to God's will, he gave her the miraculous ministry of "Shut up!" She learned to give Chris some spiritual space instead of constantly trying to pressure him into giving his life to Christ. This allowed Chris enough space to decide on

Christ for himself, which he eventually did. Jaque also learned to follow God's instructions to submit to Chris as the head of the home. This was not easy for her take-charge personality, but she now values the spiritual wisdom and strength that she sees demonstrated in Chris's quiet Phlegmatic ways.

Jaque is now Chris's favorite Bible teacher, and both have realized the power of love's transformation. God opened the door for them to learn about the personalities, and their marriage has never been the same. Now that they share a common faith and both live under the lordship of Christ, they know that God is working his will in them.

What a difference God made in Jaque and Chris's marriage and all because Jaque has learned that sometimes she just needs the ministry of "Shut up!" Overcoming her Choleric tendencies and learning to submit to Chris has enriched their marriage far beyond what either dreamed. Jaque recently wrote about the whole experience and concluded by saying, "In the end it turns out that the people Chris and I are today are the very same people we've been hoping to be married to all along!"

If you are married to a Choleric, you are sure to enjoy a home filled with projects and activities. You will have to give special attention to their needs for appreciation, action, leadership, and control. And you may have to help polish some of their rough corners. But never forget what a blessing it is to have a hard-working and quick-thinking spouse to keep your family motivated. God knew that you would need this special Choleric person in your life.

seven

THE FRET OF THE PHLEGMATIC

Wake Me When It's Over

Carol's husband taxes his mind all day programming computer secrets for the government. By nightfall he puts his mind to bed and watches TV. Since watching Carol leaping through the house exhausts him, he has learned to tune her out and put himself firmly into the quiz shows on the tube. He keeps mental note of how much he would have won if he had been the contestant. "Why don't you really go and get on one of these things?" Carol asks.

"What things?" he replies, seeming to have lost contact with her.

Carol used to get his attention by standing between him and the TV in a sexy peignoir. When that wore off she tried appearing naked, but he gently said, "Would you please move, dear, you're blocking my view." Now she's found the only way to get a rise out of him is to head toward the patio with a large chain saw. He raises one eyebrow (this takes half the energy of raising two) and asks, "What are you planning to cut up today?"

Does Carol's husband remind you of your own spouse? If you've ever found yourself going to extremes in order to get your spouse moving, you are probably married to a Phlegmatic.

Phlegmatics have nothing they feel compelled to do, and even if everyone else does nothing too, they will still be content. They have a low energy level and crave peace and quiet. They also hate confrontation and would prefer to quietly bear pain than to air their feelings and cause any conflict.

Phlegmatics enjoy being with people who will make decisions for them because they have such a hard time making decisions for themselves. If you recognize their strengths and give them respect and try not to ignore their quiet ways, they will be your best friend.

People who push the Phlegmatic around may not hear much of a response from this peaceful personality, but Phlegmatics will quietly resent their attitude. They don't like personalities that are pushy, loud, or that demand a lot of activity and work from them.

If you're married to a Phlegmatic, you will have a unique challenge and joy in living with this personality. This chapter is dedicated to exploring the Phlegmatic personality and helping you learn how to live with one.

Phlegmatic Emotional Needs

The Phlegmatic's basic desire is to have peace in life. They avoid arguments, don't like to make decisions, and flee from controversy. It's peace and quiet at all costs. Unlike the other personalities, the Phlegmatic needs special attention devoted to their self-esteem and significance.

To motivate your Phlegmatic spouse and help them be more assertive, you must learn how to fill their emotional needs. As they develop the confidence and control that is strengthened by your love and care, this personality will grow into a quietly strong leader. The following list will give you some tips on meeting the Phlegmatic's deepest needs.

1. **Peace:** Phlegmatics want peace and lack of pressure. Opposite of the Choleric who wants constant action and functions best under pressure, the Phlegmatic needs at least occasional rest. Their subconscious mind is always looking for a chair. "If I could just sit down for a few minutes . . ." When pushed into drastic action, they sometimes freeze and become immobile   so don't push. If you want them to get moving, make it sound easy and let them know you'll be at their side to help. Kind coaxing will yield dividends. Yelling produces paralysis. This person isn't lazy; they just don't like pressure and won't choose to work if given an option.

2. **Self-Worth:** The Phlegmatic needs a sense of self-worth. Often they have grown up in a home where they tended to be ignored by a parent who had to attend to the more demanding children. This passive family role created negative feelings as the child grew up and may have damaged their sense of self-worth. They've learned not to rock the boat. They aren't cute like the Sanguine, they don't mouth off at people like the Choleric, and they don't get Melancholy emotional. Instead, they stuff it all down and pretend to be happy. When you marry this person, you won't get feelings, actions, or opinions upon demand. You'll hear them say, "I don't care," "It doesn't matter," and "Whatever you feel like doing." But they really do care and need someone to build up their sense of self-worth by encouraging them to share their true feelings.

3. **Significance:** Phlegmatics need significance and inclusion. Because they stay aloof and out of trouble, they get less attention than the others   less negative attention and less positive attention. While being somewhat ignored makes life peaceful, it also instills a feeling of insignificance. As

one said to me, "I've always felt like I was just a piece of the furniture." This person needs to be included in family decisions and conversations even if he or she doesn't seem to care. Listen to their opinions and don't interrupt or shrug off their comments. Because they spend so much time observing others, they have the time to notice. Make this person feel worthwhile and not like just another piece of the furniture.

If you're a Phlegmatic, keep in mind that these needs may be hard for others to see when you don't talk about them. Your quiet personality keeps you at peace with others, but it can also prevent them from understanding you. Challenge yourself to communicate these needs to others. Talking your needs over with your spouse may cause some conflict at times, but you will find a more meaningful peace when you've worked through your differences.

Nothing's Burning in Here

Phlegmatic personalities are set apart by their easygoing nature. Nothing seems to shake this person into action. And a Phlegmatic's spouse is sure to stand amazed at some of the crazy situations a Phlegmatic can calmly sit through.

As I entered my office one morning, I saw all the Sanguine girls giggling in a group. When they looked up at me, they cried out in unison, "Wait until you hear!"

"Hear what?"

"What Jeff did."

Jeff was our resident Phlegmatic in an office full of Sanguine girls. Jeff was my husband, Fred's, favorite because he agreed with everything Fred said and was respectful to a fault.

Talking on top of each other, the girls told me the story. When they came in that morning they smelled something burning in

Jeff's office. One went in and asked, "Is there anything burning in here, Jeff?"

He looked calmly around and answered, "There's nothing burning in here."

She left but the smell got worse. "Are you *sure* there's nothing burning in here?"

Another look around and then, "There's nothing burning in here."

When the smell persisted, Choleric Karen, followed by the Sanguine contingent, walked in, passed Jeff's desk, and looked down where he sat. His leg was up against the space heater and his pant leg was on fire! The girls screamed as Jeff got up, leaving a pile of black ashes on the floor and the smell of burned polyester. Only a peaceful Phlegmatic could sit quietly in his office with his pants on fire and not notice it!

True to his low-key personality, he later offered me his half-burned-up pants. "I thought you could use them as a visual aid when you tell this story."

I do tell this story and since Jeff takes care of our book table, I often bring him up to the stage and introduce him as the one with his pants on fire. He loves the applause, and he has become his own visual aid.

A Feeling of Worth

Choleric men functioning without knowledge assume that it is their right to speak the truth, with or without love. No matter how it may hurt their mate, they say with conviction, "Surely you want to know the truth!" Unfortunately, this tendency is especially damaging to a Phlegmatic spouse.

Katie is a Phlegmatic wife married to an honest, up-front Choleric. From childhood, Katie felt herself as a quiet misfit in an aggressive family. She was excited when dynamic John chose her out of the more glamorous girls in her class. "I had always felt unappreciated and even invisible. I thought marriage would change all that because John told me he loved me."

Katie counted on two things that didn't happen after marriage. One, that she would change her feelings of low self-worth, and two, that John would continue to lift her up. The reverse happened. He made critical comments, and she sank further into a sea of worthlessness.

Since the most desperate emotional need of the Phlegmatic is a feeling of worth, you can imagine how she felt when she appeared in a new, bright-flowered, size fourteen dress and stood before him, looking for approval. He glanced her way and stated his perception of truth. "Don't you know that people your size should try to be inconspicuous?"

Katie wrote, "With those words, he took my feelings of worthlessness and turned them into fact."

How many couples, who meant well in the beginning, have failed to understand their partner's emotional needs and have therefore failed to meet them? If you are married to a Phlegmatic, remember that your well-intentioned advice can be devastating to your spouse's self-esteem. Think before you speak and make sure your praises far outnumber your criticisms.

The Phantom Patio

When Carol and Gordon bought their traditional colonial house outside of Washington, D.C., Carol planned the landscaping and bought little fresh-faced pansies and flowered shrubs. The backyard sloped down sharply so that if you opened the dining room door and stepped out, you would drop five feet and probably break your leg. As their children were growing up, Carol was afraid one of them would unlock the door and they'd all disappear. Every time Carol would bring up the possibility of losing all the children, Gordon would assure her that he was going to do something about that drop once he had it all planned out in his head. There was no rush (Phlegmatic), and he wanted it to be perfect (Melancholy). Many men of this combination spend so much time in creative thinking that they have no energy left to do the job. In most cases, this excuse of endless thinking is a stall, which may well never move into action.

Every spring, Carol would bring up the subject of the five-foot drop. "What if company was here and it was dark out and someone stepped out and fell to the ground?" Gordon calmly gave the answer, "Only have company in the daytime when they can see." Phlegmatics have a dry sense of humor and simple answers to complex problems.

To show good intentions, Gordon planted tiny Italian spruce trees around the edge of where the patio would someday be. He measured carefully how big the patio would be, taking into consideration the potential growth ratio of the wispy trees that would ultimately surround what Carol named the Phantom Patio. As the children became teenagers, they dragged a picnic table over to the spot under the sliding glass door where Carol knew people might plummet to their death. They backed the table against the outside wall and put the bench in front of it, creating large steps from the house to the yard. Weeds soon grew around the table legs, solidifying its position and ceasing any urgency to make permanent stairs.

For seventeen years Carol lived with the Phantom Patio and developed a comedy routine to explain the odd picnic-table porch to company. Gordon would listen to her story, smile and nod, but do nothing to change the situation. "If I fixed it, you'd have nothing to talk about."

But in this seventeenth year their daughter was getting married, and she wanted the reception in their backyard. She told Gordon he had to do something about that tacky table. She was not about to lose the flower girl over the edge. With no further urging, Gordon had a cedar deck built out from the door, with steps going down to the lawn. The overgrown trees outlining the

Phantom Patio were pruned back, flowers were planted for instant beauty, and the wedding reception was underway.

Later Gordon bought a hammock for the deck and said to Carol, "We should have built this a long time ago. It's a great place to just lie around and think."

Carol clapped her hand over her mouth and somehow refrained from screaming.

Different Isn't Wrong

Phlegmatics tend to make slow, methodical decisions, which can annoy the other personalities. Sanguines and Cholerics especially struggle with Phlegmatic spouses because they are used to making quick and headstrong decisions. In a marriage where these personalities meet, it becomes very easy for Phlegmatics to give up all decision-making to their more powerful and lively spouse.

Tonnie was a young, naïve Phlegmatic attending college when she met Shawn, a sensational Sanguine/Choleric pacesetter. She was overwhelmed with his exciting personality and the fact that all the girls were crazy about him. He loved her wide-eyed adoration and the way she hung on his every word. She was a popular majorette who wore miniskirts and had gorgeous legs!

Their relationship escalated, and after a few ups and downs, they were married at the age of nineteen. After the wedding, Shawn refused to allow his new wife to wear anything in public that he considered too revealing or provocative. "Your legs are for my eyes only," he said. Tonnie was astonished at this sudden change of attitude and wondered if Shawn would become controlling over everything in her life. This experience gave them both their first taste of how different they were.

These different approaches to daily life became more apparent as time went on. Phlegmatic Tonnie's idea of relaxing was to stretch out and read a book. Shawn, not understanding that this was part of her personality, thought she was lazy. Tonnie began to think he was mean because he dragged her to places with lots of activity and people when she just wanted to rest.

Another area of contention arose over Tonnie's appearance. Shawn had always wanted his wife to look like a model, and it had been Tonnie's looks that attracted him to her in the first place. For medical reasons, Tonnie's doctor placed her on birth control pills, which caused her to gain weight. Shawn's constant harping about this weight gain became a major source of conflict for the two. As a Phlegmatic, Tonnie needed to be given a feeling of self-worth. Instead, she began to feel inferior and unloved.

Avoiding outward conflict, Tonnie did what many Phlegmatics do   she become quietly stubborn. She figured that if Shawn no longer loved her, why should she bother trying to stay thin? And so she continued to gain weight. As time went by, Tonnie realized that this reaction wasn't right, but she didn't know what else to do. Both she and Shawn were young and immature, with no idea about the other's emotional needs.

Tonnie's medical problems continued, and she became more and more passive in their marriage as time passed. As a Phlegmatic, she had always struggled with making decisions. Now she just relegated all decisions to her husband because it was easier and minimized the conflicts. Underneath the surface, she continued to feel unsure of herself, and allowing Shawn to control her life with all the decision-making didn't help her self-esteem.

In the midst of these stressful times, Tonnie found out she was pregnant. She didn't know how she would handle the stress of a baby when she was in such a delicate state of mind. How could they possibly handle the care of a baby?

When their first child was born, both Tonnie and Shawn were forced to grow up and face reality. Their church began some marriage classes and started teaching Personality Plus to young married couples. Through these classes, Tonnie and Shawn had fun learning why they were different and why it had led to problems in their marriage.

For years, Tonnie had been assuming guilt for all of the problems in their marriage. She was the one gaining the weight and she was the one who couldn't make any decisions. And Shawn had been quick to agree that everything was her fault. Learning about the personalities helped them to recognize that both of their weaknesses had contributed to the breakdown in their marriage.

Tonnie is now a confident Phlegmatic with a husband who understands her emotional need for self-worth. She has learned to assert her thoughts and feelings while interacting with others, and she is now able to make mature decisions when she has to. Choleric Shawn has learned how important it is to be patient with his Phlegmatic wife and now sees that his forceful personality can be a thorn in their marriage if he doesn't learn to control it.

Some couples spend their whole marriage establishing blame. Like Tonnie, Phlegmatics often become the victim of this blame game, taking on the guilt for all the problems in their marriage. But it's hard for Phlegmatics to love someone whose main interest is making sure the Phlegmatic is the wrong one.

Understanding the personalities puts an end to the blame game. Having different personalities doesn't make either of you wrong. And your Phlegmatic spouse especially needs you to avoid dwelling on their weaknesses. Tell your Phlegmatic spouse that you love and value their unique personality   and tell them often.

Land Mines

It's been said that opposites attract, and when applied to a marriage, people need perseverance and patience to live in harmony. When an intense Choleric marries a gentle Phlegmatic, the end result is conflict, with the Choleric wanting to make the final decision while controlling the circumstances.

If you are a Phlegmatic, it's especially important for you to understand the Choleric personality. Learning how to deal with this personality in a healthy way will save you from a marriage in which your spouse takes complete control over you. Unless you recognize their strengths and weaknesses, you will live in silent resentment and rebellion.

Cindy is a sweet Phlegmatic who longed for peace and consistency in daily life and tried to keep her emotions hidden. Her husband, Sam, is a headstrong Choleric who flourishes in a fast-paced work environment and thinks he is never wrong.

Cindy describes their tumultuous years of marriage as a "war zone" with daily explosions, eruptions, and tiptoeing around the land mines. But she had resolved to stay in the marriage, to obey God, and to survive on a day-to-day basis. But as a Phlegmatic, she avoided any conflict and lived in continual hurt, pain, and confusion.

Cindy felt Sam was wrong most of the time because he had to have everything done his way, his temper was explosive, and he loved to have the last word. "In general, I didn't think he cared about me or marriage," Cindy said. He showed complete disrespect for other people. She, on the other hand, was calm, cool, and collected; kindness and sympathy were her trademarks. "In other words," she concluded, "my actions were right and his wrong."

Cindy and her three sons raged the war against her husband. They didn't understand him and felt they were justified in their attacks against him because, in their minds, he was always wrong. "He was a jerk!" Cindy explains. "Why couldn't he treat us nice? He was not worthy of any respect from the family."

After years of numbness in the marriage, Cindy was invited to a Bible study on the personalities. She didn't think it would help but decided to attend anyway. She explains, "Every chapter opened my eyes, and I began to change. A lightbulb came on and I realized Sam's different personality wasn't wrong."

Cindy made some new discoveries about her husband and herself. For the first time, her eyes were opened to the knowledge that people were created in the image of God, and each individual has a unique blueprint or personality. Cindy began to see that she and Sam were completely opposite personalities and could each be right in different ways.

In the past, her Phlegmatic personality had avoided any direct conflict with Sam. But she had often used subtle sarcasm and criticism in front of people to hurt him. She wonders now what she hoped to achieve by doing this. Neither one of them knew how to discuss anything.

Now that she understands her own Phlegmatic weaknesses, she has learned to share her feelings with him in a loving manner. Cindy has learned not to take his words and actions personally but rather to confront him in a concise and nonthreatening manner. She has learned to pick her battles by asking herself, "Will this really matter a month from now?"

Understanding the different personality traits has helped their relationship tremendously. Cindy now understands that having the last word in a discussion represents "victory" in Sam's mind. So why not let him have his victory? Cindy doesn't have the need to make the final decision, and it doesn't matter to her one way or another. This is a small concession she made to keep the peace.

Cindy also realized that her war-zone marriage modeled for her children that fighting and criticism were both normal family behaviors. When they saw the change in Cindy, this allowed them to love their father, without feeling guilty. Cindy taught them that God loves us all unconditionally and that's how we should love each other.

Cindy has learned to love her husband as he is, both strengths and weaknesses. She now appreciates Sam's strength for keeping their household under control. And she has overcome her Phlegmatic weaknesses so that she can stand up to him when important issues arise. Cindy now counts her blessings as she walks through the "land mines" in her marriage and finds refuge in the peace zone at the other side.

Forget the Stress . . . Enjoy the Mess!

The easygoing nature of Phlegmatics is not only seen in their relaxed personality but also in their surroundings. They like their worlds easily accessible with everything at their fingertips, even if they can't find it. Unlike the Melancholy who has a place for everything and everything in its place, the Phlegmatic has everything all over the place!

Janice is a peaceful Phlegmatic who was raised in a home with a Sanguine father and Choleric/Melancholy mother. Her happy-go-lucky dad was forever throwing parties and inviting the entire church over for a cookout. After the invitation was extended, her Choleric/Melancholy mom would fly into a frenzy, working Janice to death in order to get ready for the big event. As the guests arrived, Janice would retreat to her room with a plate of food in hand, hoping that staying out of sight would save her from cleaning up the remnants of the party.

Janice spent her entire childhood exhausted, trying to be a cute, outgoing Sanguine for her father and an organized, administrative Choleric/Melancholy for her mother. Typical of a Phlegmatic, she always aimed to please her parents in order to keep peace in the family.

Once Janice went away to college, she breathed a sigh of relief, feeling she could finally be herself for the first time in her life. She would do what she wanted, when she wanted, if she wanted. Her dorm room was a cluttered mess, but Phlegmatic Janice was pleasantly at rest.

One afternoon she heard a rap on the door, opened it, and found the dorm custodian, Keith, standing in the doorway. Keith was a mild-mannered man with a soothing, gentle voice.

"Hi, I'm here to check the smoke detector in your room. I know the notice said I'd be by yesterday, but I apologize—I just didn't get around to it."

Janice, not knowing if she'd ever received the notice but figuring it was buried on the shelf with a thousand other papers, replied, "That's okay; please come in, if you can get in."

Keith didn't notice the mess because it reminded him of his own apartment. He strolled in and changed the battery on the smoke detector. That was the beginning of a serene Phlegmatic relationship between the two.

Keith and Janice have been married for more than ten years now. Their marriage, like many others, has not made it this long without its ups and downs. Although they have had some marital problems, rarely do these two Phlegmatics have arguments. Their problems arise from lack of communication and motivation. For instance, managing the finances was something they both avoided at all costs, and when it came to cleaning the house and mowing the yard, they were each in full agreement that "We'll do it tomorrow." They were very active in the church and always peaceably agreed to do whatever was asked of them, but when it came to following through, neither one remembered the day or time or what they had agreed to do.

To friends and family their life seemed like an unorganized, undisciplined mess, but to two easy-does-it Phlegmatics, they were too comfortable in their relationship to notice.

All in all their life seemed simple and uncomplicated, until the day came when they had their new car repossessed. Both had signed the sales contract and both expected the other to make the payments. But they had neglected the unopened late notices, carelessly tossing them aside, waiting to read them on another day. This was the eye-opening experience that led Keith and Janice to seek help in their marriage partnership.

It was then that Keith and Janice were formally introduced to the personalities. They had always recognized that they were similar in their likes and dislikes but had never given much thought to the fact that they shared the same strengths and weaknesses. They were so preoccupied with avoiding work and watching TV that neither had ever noticed that there was no one left to take care of the basic household responsibilities.

The knowledge of the personalities gave them the necessary tools they needed to get their finances and housework in order. They hired an accountant to handle their finances, and they decluttered and systemically organized their home so it could be easily cared for with minimal effort. As far as their church commitments go, now whenever they commit to something, they ask the other party to help them out by calling and reminding them a day or two in advance.

So now even though the house isn't perfect and the lawn has many weeds, the finances are under control and the car is in the driveway!

A Surprise from Bill

Sara Jean grew up as a lone Phlegmatic child in a household of raging Cholerics, learning early that to survive she would have to dress her timid sheep-self in a wolf's clothing. When Phlegmatics have to assume Choleric behavior that does not come naturally, they often pick up many of the weaknesses as well as the strengths. Little Sara Jean learned at an early age to yell and scream to get anyone to respond to her. If she didn't make noise, she was ignored.

Masking her Phlegmatic tendencies all her life and dying inside for peace, Sara Jean married Tom, a handsome Phlegmatic man who gave her no problem, but gave her no leadership either. Sara Jean convinced herself that she was sufficiently content because at least there was no fighting   except with her children. With no healthy role models to show her differently, Sara Jean continued the parenting style she'd experienced as a girl, engaging in loud scream-fests with her Choleric children and trying to keep up with their argumentative, aggressive ways. Like so many Phlegmatics, Sara Jean could not win. She was exhausted, the kids were in control, and Dad was in the other room, hoping the fighting would stop.

Phlegmatic Tom knew that he should provide some leadership, especially when he watched his children defy the household rules and dishonor their mother, but he just didn't know how. Tom privately sent away for a videotape on male leadership, and listened to some Personality Plus tapes a friend at church had given him. One day, after their twelve-year-old daughter, Lisa, had expertly tongue-lashed her tired mother, Tom walked into the room and told the two of them to shut up and sit down. Both Sara Jean and Lisa were surprised to see Tom involving himself in what he normally called "typical female stuff." They waited to see what normally passive Tom had to say.

In a firm tone he told his daughter, "Honey, you do not have to obey the household rules or treat your mother with respect . . . if you want to live elsewhere. But if you live here under our roof, you will obey the rules and treat your mother with honor, or you will have to cook your own dinner, do your own laundry, get yourself to school, and lose all phone and TV privileges. Starting today. Is that clear?" Sara Jean was relieved to finally have her husband stand up and set healthy boundaries with the kids, and she relaxed a little in her chair.

Lisa immediately replied, "You can't make me!"

Tom quickly replied, "You're right. I can't make you. You have choices. You're too big to spank, but I can make sure life is difficult for you if you continue to choose selfishness and disrespect in our home. This woman is my wife, and no one will talk to her the way you have anymore. I love you too much to let you keep acting like a spoiled brat."

Lisa sat there with her mouth hanging open. She'd never heard her father speak to her that way. Then Tom surprised them both.

He turned to his wife, put his face close to hers, and said, "And I expect you to quit allowing your daughter to disrespect you. She can only do it if you let her, Sara Jean. I don't want you to take it anymore. Will you please honor and respect yourself enough to do that?" With that, a stunned Sara Jean watched her husband quietly pick up the newspaper and head back out to the porch.

Shocked that her husband had reprimanded her as well as her daughter, Sara Jean also felt relief that he had taken the leadership role. Warm, close feelings crept into her heart toward the man to whom she had lately been cool and distant.

Because Tom was willing to speak up and take a stand against an out-of-control Choleric, setting boundaries in a quiet, firm way, Sara Jean responded by agreeing to do the same. With time, Sara Jean and Tom began to take turns carrying the burden of leadership in their home, something which was not always comfortable to either one of them, but at which they persisted and eventually learned quite well.

As this story illustrates, Phlegmatics are not incapable of leading or standing up for themselves and others. They are usually slower to anger and wait until there is a crisis to act, hoping someone else will solve the situation or that it will all go away.

With that understanding, we as parents should help train our Phlegmatic children early on to assume leadership roles they will need in their own marriage and family relationships. And if you have a Phlegmatic spouse, you may have to nudge them into the leadership positions they tend to avoid. With the proper education, especially understanding the personalities, Phlegmatics can make great leaders, as long as their endless patience does not stretch into endless avoidance.

A Tribute to a Phlegmatic

Leslie Vernick is author of several books, including *The Truth Principle*. She is a licensed clinical social worker and uses the knowledge of the personalities as a tool in helping her understand some of her problem cases. Recently, she shared with me a touching story of how childhood trauma had influenced her adult decision to marry a peaceful Phlegmatic.

Just before Leslie and her husband, Howard, celebrated their twenty-fifth wedding anniversary, one of Leslie's friends posed this question: "If you could change anything about your husband, what would it be?" As Leslie pondered that question, she thought about how at times she wished her husband was more fun.

Howard and Leslie were both first-born children, high achievers, and serious minded. Neither one scored a single point in the Sanguine column of the Personality Profile. She was a fairly even mix of Melancholy and Choleric; he was mostly Phlegmatic with just a touch of Melancholy. Rip-roaring belly laughter was never something that they generated very easily. They could have fun together, but they always needed an outside catalyst to get their fires burning.

As Leslie reflected on this, however, she realized how much she would miss her husband's Phlegmatic steadiness and peaceful attitude if he were to suddenly become more fun. Howard wasn't the type to get moody or emotional   he was very predictable. And while some folks might find those qualities boring, Leslie found them comforting because they met her Melancholy needs for security and stability.

As she thought more about her marriage, she realized that each of her Choleric/Sanguine siblings had also married a Phlegmatic spouse. As a licensed clinical social worker, she began to wonder if there was anything in their shared childhood that contributed to them each choosing this type of life partner.

"Our parents were divorced when I was eight years old," Leslie explained. "My sister was four and my brother just two." Leslie's life became chaotic and very unpredictable after her parents' divorce. Sometimes her mom didn't come home after work, and she and her siblings didn't know where she was. Other times, she would be in a bad mood, and they would stay out of her way, playing outside until dark and then sneaking quietly back into the house. Her mom would occasionally surprise them with wonderful weekends away, but most of the time money was tight.

As Leslie and her siblings got a little older, they learned to swipe empty cartons of soda bottles off the back porches of other apartments, cashing in the two-cent refund so they could buy food. Candy and French fries were the preferred meals. Although these treats were not nutritious, they filled Leslie and her siblings' empty bellies when the fridge was bare.

When Leslie reached her early teen years, she and her brother and sister were removed from their mother's home and court-ordered to live with their father and stepmother. Life became much more stable and predictable. Home was finally a safe place for them.

"As adults," Leslie shares, "I think each of us chose a Phlegmatic partner not only because it complements our natural temperament but because of our early childhood experiences." She goes on to explain how they intuitively knew that they would do best with a spouse who was steady and calm and would not bring them back to the anxiety of their youth. "I think we made good choices!" Leslie now says after over twenty-five years of marriage, "None of us has divorced or even separated."

Melancholy Leslie treasures her Phlegmatic husband. Sure, there are times she wishes Howard were more outgoing and spontaneous, but she would not trade this steady guy for all the excitement in the world.

If you are married to a Phlegmatic, you too will find yourself treasuring the stability and quiet strengths of your spouse. Even though their lack of motivation and activity may frustrate you at times, always remember to build up their self-worth and give them the peaceful moments they need. In his perfect plan, God has blessed you with this easygoing and thoughtful spouse to cherish for a lifetime.

PART 3
Making Music Together

Dynamics of the Personalities

eight

DIFFERENT SCALES, SCRIPTS, AND SCENES

When You Marry Your Opposite

Since Fred and I started working with couples in 1966, we have found that by nature we marry individuals who are opposite to our own personality. We fall in love with opposite strengths and go home to live with opposite weaknesses. Then we set out to change our mate to be wonderful, "like me!"

The flighty, fun-loving Sanguine woman falls for the deep, organized, serious Melancholy man with his calendars and daily planners. After a while she starts to buck his list of duties. "This is no fun." And he loves her ability to talk to anyone about anything—until he sees that she talks constantly to anyone in sight and half of what she says is lies.

The super-achieving Choleric woman can do more in a given day than several of her friends put together. She falls in love with a Phlegmatic man who has a quiet sense of humor and no compulsive behaviors. "He's so peaceful!" she says, until she realizes he may be *too* peaceful for her liking. And he likes her take-charge attitude and is relieved he no longer has to make decisions. But after a while he gets tired of being bossed around and feeling like his opinion doesn't count. "Don't I have a vote here?"

Couples with opposite personalities face both unique joys and unique challenges. When a spouse's strengths cover up the weaknesses of their partner, we see these combinations shining at their best. But when two spouses' strengths are carried to the extreme, they often become weaknesses. If couples aren't prepared for these weaknesses, their marriage may quickly go out of tune.

When Strengths Become Weaknesses

If we could meet with each couple before they marry, we could give them a realistic view of what their future will be like. But young people in love don't want anyone to rain on their parade. They are convinced they were made for each other and are ready to live happily ever after.

Unfortunately for many, they are unprepared for each other's personalities. They don't realize that what they found appealing in their spouse before marriage can begin to annoy them shortly thereafter. The stresses and strains of living with their opposite often cause spouses' strengths to turn into weaknesses.

Ruth is a beautiful, soft-spoken Phlegmatic who married an energetic Choleric. She met her husband at a college/career Christmas party at church. Ironically, she had just convinced herself that morning that she was going to put away her "What I desire in a mate" checklist and just enjoy life. She was twenty-four and had grown tired of waiting around for something that could take years to manifest.

With that in mind, she went to the Christmas party, and wouldn't you know it, that's when her future husband walked in—6′4″, brown hair, and the bluest eyes she had ever seen. Fresh off his boat, the USS *Downs*, he was home for Christmas break visiting his family.

Ruth remembers her very first thought after seeing him: "Oh, my, is *he* the one?" After a brief introduction and a few moments of nervous conversation, she went back to making hot cider and spent the rest of the evening feeling like a teenager. Every time she left the room, he followed her, if not in person, then with his dazzling blue eyes. Little did Ruth know that Matt had seen her across the sanctuary nearly four months earlier and had been waiting ever since to make his move!

Needless to say, their relationship started that night. His handsome features and charm baited her. But it was his recent conversion to Christ and his desire to learn more about God that kept her nibbling. After a few weeks of long-distance courting (he lived in San Diego and she in Los Angeles), she knew that his commitment, energy, and persistence had hooked her. With similar interests in skiing and mountain biking, they were a match made in heaven.

Looking back now, Ruth sees those first days as ignorant bliss: "They say love is blind and it's true. When you are in love, the sky could be cloudy and gray and it just doesn't matter." She chose to overlook the fact that he was two years younger than her, and they wasted no time in dating. Within six months they were engaged, and they married within a year after they first met.

Fortunately, Ruth explains, they had wonderful premarital counseling and a relationship-minded aunt who gave them *After Every Wedding Comes a Marriage*. Once their honeymoon slowed down, they both read the book and found it to be a real blessing. They learned something that premarital counseling had missed, which was that despite their similarities, they were wired differently.

"In the early stages of our love," Ruth explains, "my Melancholy/Phlegmatic insecurities and indecisiveness were drowned out by Matt's Choleric/Melancholy strength and surefootedness." At that point in their relationship, she saw no signs of Matt's intolerance and lack of forethought, and neither of them knew that her compassion and lack of follow-through would be a hindrance to the way she mothered their children.

145

It took about five years into their marriage to see the change. Matt's charm began to fade into curt words. Ruth hadn't noticed before that Matt's comments and decisions were fired straight from the hip, and his need to just "get things done" could cause sloppy results. But she also came to realize that her Melancholy perfectionism could compensate for this weakness.

When Matt wanted a camper shell for his Toyota 4x4, he decided to take the money they had been saving for a vacation and buy the shell instead. The dingy red color clashed with his bright blue truck, but it didn't matter to him because the price was right. Ruth let him do his wheeling and dealing, and they headed home with the eyesore. Having the traits of a perfectionist and needing to think things through, it took Ruth a while to get the courage to express her feelings about his ridiculous purchase. Once Ruth explained how she felt, he saw that his urgency to purchase a shell was unfounded, and he took the shell back.

Ruth learned about the personality differences early in her marriage and had a husband who was willing to listen. Knowing their weaknesses from the start has helped Matt and Ruth stay accountable to one another. They can now handle the situations where their strengths turn into weaknesses and even use tough problems to grow in their love and understanding.

Like Matt and Ruth, you can stay off the hot coals and rocky cliffs by understanding that God makes each person different. If you are committed to being together forever, it is best to learn quickly how to deal with your differences. You will constantly be sanding rough edges and polishing round ones, but it will get easier every day to find the root of your differences and work towards a comfortable middle ground.

The Bible says, "My people perish from a lack of knowledge," and the same is true of marriage. As you learn more about the different personalities, you will be liberated in knowing that God has even designed our idiosyncrasies and shortcomings. It is all right to act and react a certain way. But God's strength can also help us avoid allowing our strengths to be weaknesses. As iron sharpens iron, so it is with our personalities. And a combination couple carries a special ability to complement each other's traits.

Identifying Strengths and Weaknesses

One of the best ways to prevent your strengths from turning into weaknesses is to be aware of them both. When an individual understands their own tendencies, they can work to maximize the positive and minimize the negative. Marriage provides an individual with the extra benefit of a loving spouse who can hold them accountable in this refining process.

Taking the time to identify and discuss you and your spouse's strengths and weaknesses is a valuable exercise for your marriage. When you both understand each other's strengths, you can encourage each other to use them in positive ways, gaining greater confidence in your abilities as well. When you both recognize and discuss your weaknesses, you can hold each accountable for avoiding them, rather than just being silently annoyed with each other. And a healthy awareness of your own weaknesses will prevent you from being hurt or upset when your spouse lovingly points them out to you. When both spouses have this healthy awareness, they become a team working to build each other up rather than two individuals who pull each other down.

The following lists show some appealing traits that attract us to our spouse before marriage and what those characteristics may turn into when left unchecked. As we've already discussed, strengths carried to extremes become our weaknesses. Take some time to look at the strengths and weaknesses of you and your spouse's personality types and talk about them together. Are there certain strengths and weaknesses that seem to particularly apply to you? What can your spouse do to help you maximize those strengths and minimize those weaknesses?

147

SANGUINE

Strengths:	Weaknesses:
Storytelling	Exaggeration
Colorful descriptions	Lies
Commanding voice	Loud mouth
Friendly nature	Talks to anyone
Free thinker	Undisciplined
Casual attitude	No sense of time
Unworried, unhurried	Late for everything
Loves to shop	Overspends, in debt
Generous	Gives to everyone
Optimistic	Can't think ahead
Spontaneous	Never plans
Magnetic personality	Fills the house up

MELANCHOLY

Strengths:	Weaknesses:
Neat and meticulous	Obsessive neatness
Money manager	Stingy
Deep thinker	Won't talk
Introspective	Brooding
Serious mind	Depressed
Plans ahead	No spontaneity
Persistent	Won't give up
Sensitive	Easily hurt
Analytical	Takes forever
Idealistic	Out of touch
Detailed	Nit-picking
Long-term memory	Unforgiving

CHOLERIC

Strengths:	Weaknesses:
Strong leader	Bossy
Quick thinker	Foolhardy decisions
Good at business	Takes impulsive steps
Works hard	Becomes workaholic
Persuasive	Con artist
Strong-willed	Stubborn
Competitive	Must win
Self-reliant	Doesn't need you
Straight talk	Insulting
Fast decisions	Impatient

PHLEGMATIC

Strengths:	Weaknesses:
Easygoing	Lazy
Peaceful	Not exciting
Enjoys good TV	Watches anything
Appears to listen	Tunes you out
Smiles and nods	Doesn't hear a word
Cool, detached look	Is detached
Consistent	Stuck in a rut
Adaptable	Indecisive
Soft, low voice	Mumbles
Fits in anywhere	Lost in the crowd
Balanced thinker	No opinion
Seductive look	Too tired

149

He's Not Out to Get Me

When two different personalities come together in marriage, the potential for misunderstanding is high. What the Sanguine spouse intends as a lighthearted joke may be felt as a barbed arrow piercing a Melancholy's heart. The Choleric's assumption that everyone wants to work as hard as he does may be seen by their low-key, Phlegmatic spouse as an intentional effort to make them feel inadequate.

Such misunderstandings usually start out as seemingly small and insignificant. Over time, however, these misunderstandings can grow. And when spouses fail to understand each other's personalities, these conflicts may develop into permanent resentment or fear.

Shirley met Nate in high school during the 1950s. With the war finally over, all were optimistic. The allies had defeated Hitler, the troops were coming home, and many couples planned to get married and live happily ever after. TV added to these expectations with its depictions of sweet little families where Mother stayed home to raise the precious children. In real life, most women expected their husbands to earn the money, while they raised the family and created a peaceful home.

This time in history is called the Baby Boomer years, and Shirley did her part by producing four children in four and a half years. Her husband became an officer in the Air Force and looked at his burgeoning family as another unit to control. Neither Nate nor Shirley understood the personalities, and each one expected the other to think and function like them.

Because of his position, Nate had many social obligations that he considered business necessities. As a Choleric, he wanted to do the right things, go to the right parties, speak to all the right people, and then get out of there. Shirley, burdened at home with four young children, looked at these parties as her Sanguine escape to fun. She would dress up, tell stories to all who would listen, and eat everything in sight. Those parties were her big moments. As she was just warming up, Nate would be finishing his business and telling her, "I've done what I came to do, so I can leave." Spending the night on needless charm and small talk seemed like a waste of time once his obligation had been filled.

Shirley could tell her moments of sociability were nearing an end when she saw him heading across the room with a determined look. Shirley would go home in tears like Cinderella yanked away from the ball before midnight. Nate would be angry that she was whimpering over his fulfilling an obligation that had nothing to do with her. "Be grateful I took you at all!" was his frequent response to her tears.

He couldn't see why she wanted to stay at such a boring event. She couldn't see why he wanted to leave such a fun party. Neither one of these intelligent people could understand the other's way of thinking. And both would end up feeling like the other one was out to get them.

Before they learned about their personality differences, these scenes would often repeat themselves. Nate's need to control and fix things often interfered with Shirley's need for acceptance and approval. He focused on "what's next" while she tried to get attention and have fun. For thirty years Shirley saw his "controlling, fix-it" personality as a threat to her fun-loving, "who cares as long as everyone is happy" Sanguine personality. She wanted affection and attention, which were difficult needs for the Choleric to understand or give. Nate's need to be in charge and to fix things created feelings of inadequacy in Shirley, and simply left her feeling unloved.

Since learning about the personalities, Shirley and Nate's resentments have receded. Instead of expecting the other person to be just like them, they have learned to appreciate each other's differences. And most importantly, seeing the other person's perspective has helped them both understand that they aren't out to get each other.

Different People, Different Needs

One of the greatest blessings in understanding the personalities is being able to better meet each other's needs. You are more likely to build up romantic love when you deal with your mate out of their personality rather than your own. When you reach out to your mate at their level, they can better understand your expressions of love. This then enables your spouse to appreciate your actions and respond to what you say.

For couples with opposite personalities, this is especially important. Otherwise, both spouses exhaust themselves trying to show love in ways that the other spouse just doesn't understand. The logical Choleric may feel like they are helping their spouse by dissecting a problem and then trying to fix it. But if their Sanguine spouse simply wants someone to listen to their story, they will feel that their needs are unmet.

Instead, these spouses need to recognize their different needs and stop expecting the other to be like them. The idea of showing your spouse love in a way that you yourself would not respond to takes some getting used to. But it sure pays off. Not only will you find yourselves more effective at meeting each other's needs, but you won't be as exhausted from your efforts!

Don't Fix It!

When Shirley developed a dental disorder know as TMJ, she suffered a great deal of pain and discomfort. One day when the pain was particularly bad, her husband came home and found her in tears. She told him of her pain and said she was going up to bed because she couldn't stand it any longer.

In his typical Choleric way, Nate immediately began his twenty questions. "What's the matter? When did it start? How did it develop? What are your symptoms? What medications have you taken?" And the questions went on.

Finally, Sanguine Shirley looked at him and said, "Right now I don't care about any of those questions. I need you to sympathize with me, take me up to bed, offer me soda and crackers, put your arm around me, and say, 'I'm sorry you're in pain. Is there anything I can do to help?'"

Amazingly, her husband did just that. Ten minutes later, as he was leaving the room after tucking her in and doing all that she had asked of him, he eagerly asked, "How did I do?"

She responded, "Wonderful, thank you."

And then he acknowledged, "Do you have any idea how hard this was for me not to try and fix your problem?"

It may have been hard for Nate to stop his questioning and just help his wife to bed. After all, Cholerics would prefer to be left alone with no offers of help when they are sick. But sympathy was exactly what Shirley needed. As a Sanguine, she wanted attention, not a quick solution. In the end, Nate's willingness to respond to Shirley from her personality perspective instead of his own left them both satisfied. Shirley fell asleep feeling loved and cared for, and Nate knew that he had successfully communicated his love in a way she understood.

Growing Together

Learning to live with our opposite can lead to tremendous growth. When we realize that our spouse is not out to get us, we become free to accept their way of loving us and helping us grow. And instead of focusing all our energies on changing them, we learn to change together. A husband and wife who are committed to meeting each other's needs in this way will find themselves growing in both character and love.

Recognizing God as the creator of our personalities also provides the opportunity for spiritual growth. Psalm 139:13–16 says that God created us and knew us before we were even born. We each have strengths and weaknesses, and as we learn to see them through the eyes of our loving Father, we become better at blending them together.

A friend of mine recently shared that when she first met her husband, she was attracted to his strengths, but after they married, had children, and lived their daily lives, those strengths became irritants. Now that they understand the personalities, she is again attracted by his strong personality traits, except now she sees them as God-given strengths that she doesn't have in herself. She can now say, "I welcome those traits into our relationship, and life has become a real blessing to both of us."

Without an understanding of the personalities and a commitment to marriage, this couple may never have experienced such wonderful growth.

A Sure Foundation

When Jesus Christ becomes our marital foundation, we try to meet the needs of each other as God leads us. And the personalities are one tool he gives us for understanding our spouse. When we see that God created our spouse's personality as a complement to our own, we stop feeling threatened and begin to appreciate their strengths as a complement to our weaknesses.

Shirley and Nate have found this blessing for their marriage. Shirley no longer feels offended or guilty by Nate's Choleric drive. She now appreciates how God made him, and how he put the two of them together. Instead of trying to prove herself to Nate, she rejoices that God gave him a desire for a fun-loving, sometimes off-the-wall spouse.

Shirley spent years asking God to change Nate. She now thanks God for not listening to her prayer! She believes that God has given her something better; she says, "He gave me an understanding of who he created Nate to be and who he created me to be." She now asks God to change her and help her love Nate with Christ's unconditional love.

Nate and Shirley's success story is a wonderful reminder of what marriage rooted in Christ can be. To God be the glory and gratitude for giving us knowledge of the personalities so we can all, with his help, relate to our spouse in a godly manner. With his foundation underneath, even complete opposites can get along!

nine

IN THE SAME KEY

When You're Married to the Same Personality

Occasionally, people do marry someone who shares their personality type. This usually happens in second marriages or older marriages. Instead of using only our hearts and being emotionally drawn to those with opposite strengths, we use our minds and look for someone more like us. The result is joyful compatibility that is unique to same-personality couples.

But similar personalities also present their own set of problems. You can envision this yourself. Two Sanguines are both looking for an audience and dying for attention. Two Cholerics want to be in charge. Two Melancholies want things done perfectly but they have different sets of standards. And two Phlegmatics don't care if anything is done on time and hope the other person will do it.

Instead of fitting like a glove, this marriage is bumping heads, looking for the same response from each other. And although they enjoy double of their strengths, they also hold the potential to have double weaknesses. Without an opposite personality, there is no one to pull them back from the brink of disaster or despair. Fortunately, same-personality couples can enjoy their compatibility and avoid the pitfalls of their weaknesses if they take the time to understand the dynamics of their marriage.

If you are married to your same personality, take a few moments to look at the "Marital Balance Chart." On it you will see a brief list of the assets and liabilities in your same-personality marriage. As you read the rest of the chapter, you will learn how these assets and liabilities come into play for all four marriage types.

MARITAL BALANCE CHART
by Marita Littauer

Popular Sanguines The "Fun" Marriage	Perfect Melancholies The "Organized" Marriage
Assets:	Assets:
Spontaneous	Neat home
Exciting	Long-range plans
Enthusiastic	Financial order
Keep marriage fresh	Punctual
Flexible	Value education
Compromising	Remember important dates
Forgiving	Committed to each other
Play with children	Loving and protective of children
Liabilities:	Liabilities:
Lack of plans and goals	Critical
Unstable	Danger of midlife crisis
Flirtatious	Depressed and brooding
Messy	Keep record of wrongs
No one listens	Reinforce each other's negativity
Superficial relationship	Stuck in a routine
Fail to put down roots	May be unfaithful
Blurred generational lines (child may become the parent)	High expectations place heavy burden on relationship
Poor financial planning	

Powerful Cholerics	Peaceful Phlegmatics
The "Active" Marriage	The "Relaxed" Marriage
Assets:	Assets:
Goal-oriented	Stable
Clear boundaries	Agreeable
High accomplishments	Content
Respect each other	Low pressure
High energy	Modest
Championing causes	Patient with children
Firm parenting	Satisfied
Liabilities:	Liabilities:
Struggle for control	Low accomplishment
Overcommitted	Lack of planning or direction
No time for each other	Kids take over
Two careers pulling on marriage	Dull
Marriage is low priority	Control is passive-aggressive
Blurring of personal and professional boundaries	Lack of communication
	Loss of individual identity
Shouting contests	Blurred generational lines (child may become the parent)
Fear of sharing	
	Fear of conflict

Lots of Fun, Nothing Done—Sanguine Marries Sanguine

Two Sanguines are the most fun of any possible combination. They both have a great sense of humor and can tell hilarious stories to amuse their audience. With appreciative responses, they will feed off each other and the story will grow ever funnier. They are both great party givers and party goers, and their overwhelming desire is to have fun and double fun!

Because Sanguines desire affection and approval, they also tend to be very giving as a couple. This need for love will make them do whatever it takes to keep them popular, such as giving things away or picking up their friends' dinner tabs. Their big hearts make them bend over backwards for their friends and families.

Sanguine couples also tend to be very upbeat and optimistic. When it comes to financial needs, they are the ones who will put complete faith in God to provide. And when they face an uphill struggle together, two Sanguines can keep smiling even amidst the pain.

At their best, the Sanguine couple will be a generous pair who's always there for their friends. They will bring sparkle and laughter to any room, and they will keep each other entertained through a lifetime of spontaneous fun.

Double the Fun—Double the Debt

When two Sanguines marry, there are some obvious problems as well. They both want to have fun, and neither one wants to count the cost. They tend to be emotionally immature and remain childlike in their approach to life. This innocence is appealing, but their inability to plan ahead coupled with their lack of mature responsibility can lead to disaster.

One negative with a Sanguine combination is their double lack of responsibility. They both mean well, apologize quickly, and promise to do better tomorrow. They want so desperately to be popular that they will do whatever it takes to make others like them. Unfortunately, when these efforts go to the extreme, there is no one there to stop them. As Sanguines, they will both continue to ignore their responsibilities if it means having more fun and getting people to like them.

This irresponsibility carries over into their finances as well. Their kindhearted generosity is good, but sometimes they are like happy giving children who don't know how to count the cost until the bills arrive. Their optimism and trust in God's providence are also wonderful traits, but when they are carried to the extreme of ignoring God's wisdom in their spending habits, these strengths become faults. Instead of true confidence in God, they start to place hope in a "lucky" windfall that will help them pay the bills.

In the end, two fun-seekers tend to ignore boring budgets and financial planners. Instead, they stick to their instincts of impulsive spending for spontaneous fun. When you put two of these party-going spenders together, you can see how quickly they can get into financial disaster.

No Money! No Fun!

An ideal for a Sanguine would be to marry a millionaire and spend wildly forever. Unfortunately, I've not met a wealthy pair of Sanguines. But I have counseled Sanguine couples who have clothes, cars, and gadgets—plus a pile of depressing bills. They haven't learned that their "life is just a bowl of cherries" attitude won't work in the real world where someone has to pay for the cherries.

Ben and Melanie are both Sanguines involved in a Christian ministry before they were married. In contrast to the mostly Melancholy group that felt burdened to evangelize the entire world, these two Sanguines were happy just to make it through the day. Everyone loved them but wondered if they'd ever get their act together. Neither one of them seemed to know how to count or keep track of time, nor did they ever seem to care. Melancholy friends bailed them out and shook their collective heads. "Will they ever shape up and become responsible?"

It seemed a foregone conclusion they would marry each other and be happy (though broke) ever after. The wedding was small. There were no invitations, and they invited whatever people they ran into the weeks before. "Who knows who will show up!" They had no time or money for a regular reception, so they reserved a back section in a Mexican restaurant. Each person paid for their own food and the local mariachi band provided free music. Cheap fun!

You can probably picture the rest. They became youth pastors and had their small apartment full of teens all the time. From their Sanguine perspective, there was no point in cleaning—the appartment would only get messed up again. Sometimes Melanie would get pouty and depressed over the sad situation she lived in, so Ben would take her out for dinner and charge up some unneeded item to make her feel better. Bills piled up and there was never enough money to catch up. No fun!

Ten years later they are still treading financial water and still seeking fun. They'll get a bigger place and maybe have children someday, when they save enough money.

In contrast to Ben and Melanie, Todd and Becky thought their potential problems through ahead of time. Both Sanguines, they knew they enjoyed spending money more than saving it. He had been through bankruptcy, and she had come out of a failed marriage with severe financial problems. They determined not to make the same mistakes again.

Becky had come to one of my personality seminars, bought *Personality Plus,* and could suddenly see why they had money problems. They both spent without thinking about the future. They had good jobs with bright possibilities, but they needed to change their loose habits. They went to a financial consultant who set up schedules for them. Each month they sent their paychecks to him along with their bills, and he opened a modest savings account for them, putting in a small portion on a regular basis. At the end of each period, he would let them know how much they could spend on eating out and entertainment.

"It's the first time in my adult life I've ever felt secure," Becky told me. "I know we could do this ourselves, but experience has shown we wouldn't."

Now a few years down the line, they have saved enough for a down payment on a house. "The little cloud of impending doom has lifted," Becky reports. "We learned that spending money we didn't have to create fun we didn't need was no fun at all!"

Todd and Becky's experience provides a great example of two Sanguines who recognize their weaknesses and learn how to make the most of them. Not all Sanguines will need to hire an outside financial manager, but some attention to your financial situation will be necessary if you want to be responsible about future goals. Long-term savings may not seem like fun right now—but they can help you prevent the "no money, no fun" financial cycle that many Sanguine couples fall into.

Too Busy Looking for Affection—No Time for the Routine!

Another problem two Sanguines can encounter stems from their double need for affection and approval. They want their mate to think they are precious, adorable, charming, and magnetic. But if their mate is busy looking for the same adoration, neither one of them is apt to get it.

Even when Sanguines do learn how to give each other the affection and approval they both desire, their relationship can get them into trouble. Because Sanguines love spontaneity, gifts, and fun, these two will overspend on frequent celebrations and gifts for each other. Instead of learning how to show their love in less expensive ways, this couple just gets themselves into further financial trouble as they continue to spend money in an endless cycle.

Always seeking approval and fun, Sanguine couples also tend to ignore social responsibilities and routines that get in the way. They forget the day and time and what it was they said they'd do. They rise quickly to positions of prominence in church and social groups because of their humor and outgoing natures, but once they are there, they don't give attention to the important details. Sanguine couples enjoy preparing a special social dinner once or twice a year because they will receive praise. But they are bored with the routine of feeding the family and keeping the house. TV dinners, take-out Chinese, and home-delivered pizza were made for the Sanguine who glances at the clock and says in surprise, "Is it time to eat again?"

Can you imagine this adorable, irresponsible couple if they have children? A Sanguine child might be able to bounce along with the fun and visit friends when they need a good meal. But a Melancholy child will be depressed over the chaos and forgetfulness and become friends with the school psychologist. Phlegmatic kids will tune out the confusion and not complain until the school nurse suspects malnutrition, and the Choleric child, at an early age, will see the hopelessness of their Sanguine parents and exclaim, "Somebody's got to take charge here!"

Unless the Sanguine couple learns about these weaknesses and takes measures to avoid them, their family and their home will quickly fall into disrepair.

Buying Two of Everything

Sanguine Mary was in deep dramatic grief over the death of her Phlegmatic husband, who had been the rock of the marriage and kept their finances in order. Mary owned an antique shop that never made much money for two reasons. One, she didn't charge enough, and two, she wanted to keep everything for herself. She bought things she liked and then couldn't bear to part with them. Her husband would come in occasionally and tell her what she must sell in order to pay the rent. She would cry and carry on, but then she would do what he had quietly suggested. Once her husband died, she was beside herself. Who would handle the bills? Who would take care of her?

In the antique shop next door was the answer—a man named Andy. He was in his sixties like Mary, and as a widower he had time to give sustained sympathy to Mary. He lifted her spirits and had a stream of funny stories to assuage her grief. In a short time, Mary found that she couldn't get through a day without his sense of humor and protective arms around her. They had been friends for years, but now she looked at him in a new way.

Mary was desperate for a man and just assumed that all men were adept at finances. In reality, Howard was more like her. Even though they didn't understand the personalities, they had many things in common. They both loved collecting, shopping, visiting, eating, and laughing. They were both lonely and looking for fun. What a perfect couple. They were also both impulsive, and one day they got a great idea: "Let's get married!"

Because they had such a short courtship, Mary and Andy hadn't noticed that they shared the same weaknesses. Thus they were surprised when these weaknesses cropped up in their marriage. Mary was used to being the only shopper in the family, but now there were two. But Andy, recognizing Mary's need for gifts and approval, swept her off her feet with lots of flowers and gifts. Even after they got married, he continued with extravagant gifts that they really couldn't afford.

Like Mary, Andy liked to stop and shop. They would end up with lots of extra food and lots of extra pounds because of their frequent trips to the grocery store. They would also end up with extra cards and gifts for their grandchildren. When their grandson turned one, Howard came home and said, "I found the cutest card for Grayson's first birthday!" Mary said, "Oh, I already bought him one too; we can just send him both of them!"

Since getting married, Mary has begun to feel more stress over money. All these extra cards and gifts take their toll on the family finances, and Mary is not used to a spouse who shares her recklessness with money. Mary and Andy now seem to be sobering up to reality and learning that they can have fun without spending a lot of money. They have given up some of their collectibles and have learned to talk about the finances before offering extravagant or double gifts.

The dynamics of a Sanguine couple make it important for them to weigh their probable future actions. They need to realize that neither one of them will naturally watch their spending or take responsibility for maintaining a routine. And they must remember that their natural generosity and need for attention will lead to the natural by-product of overgiving. When these weaknesses are kept in check, Sanguines will not only enjoy a lot of fun with their mate, they will also have the means to pay for it!

Doing It Right Fills Others with Fright—
Melancholy Marries Melancholy

While the Sanguine couple is having fun, the Melancholy couple is setting up life so it will be perfect. They plan, chart, graph, study, and analyze before they move into cautious action. When Melancholies marry each other they are a serious pair. They do nothing impulsively and are dumbfounded by Sanguines who run off half-cocked without a care in the world. They admire the Choleric work ethic but see that their problems arise when they haven't planned things out ahead of time. And they are so glad they didn't marry either of them.

Everything in the double Melancholy home has its proper place and is sitting in it right now. They prefer neutral colors in decorating—that don't show the dirt or need a lot of upkeep. And their clothes will be high quality, hung neatly, and arranged by color and type in the meticulous Melancholy closet. Their finances are in order too, and they don't spend what they haven't got.

This couple is quiet, reserved, and intellectual. If they don't know the answer to a question, they have a book about it and they know exactly where it is! They both enjoy classical music and like to read deep books that will touch them intellectually and emotionally.

This obviously is the perfect couple. But can perfection ever be less than perfect? How do others view this couple?

The Compulsive Perfectionists

Compulsive means "pulled in one direction." Melancholy couples are always pulled in the direction of perfection. If a project isn't perfect, they aren't satisfied. And if their detailed daily schedule gets interrupted, they are not pleased. This need for perfection is sure to keep the Melancholy home in perfect order. But if two Melancholies are not careful, they will miss many meaningful relationships and moments in life because they spend too much time on the details.

Harold and Katheryn share a compulsive need for a constant daily pattern. As a retiree, Harold enjoys making things out of wood. Every day he goes out at about 8:00, has coffee at 10:00, goes out again until 3:00, and then stops for an early dinner. Even on Sunday mornings while waiting for Katheryn to dress, he is driven to at least go out to his woodshop to figure out what he'll do next and get sawdust on his neatly tied tie.

Every morning Katheryn has a one-hour devotional. Then at 8:00 she goes into her study, which is lighted by a perfectly beautiful crystal chandelier, and writes nearly straight through until 3:00 in the afternoon. After an early dinner she returns to writing until 8:00 in the evening. She buys books because she loves to learn. But as a compulsive perfectionist she wants to keep her library down to fifteen hundred books, so she frequently spends time sorting through the titles and deciding which ones to give away.

Katheryn and Harold also share a Melancholy sense of order. His workshop is unbelievably tidy. He has wrenches lined up on a pegboard by order of size. Look in his toolbox and you'll see screwdrivers lined up by size. Then there's his closet. Dress shirts are on apricot hangers, jersey shirts on white hangers, dress pants on brown hangers, and golf pants on red hangers.

Katheryn has her spices lined up in alphabetical order in four specially designed pullout shelves. She has shoes too numerous to count because they must match each outfit. She has eight different sets of flatware to match their abundance of dishes. Each set of place settings has its own drawer with divided sections to keep them in order. Every room is decorated in a single color with a secondary color. The bedroom is yellow with some green, the living room is black and pink, the dining room is burgundy and silver. . . . The details of this couple's ordered life go on and on!

In typical Melancholy fashion, they can both spend hours at a time working on just one thing. Fortunately, this couple doesn't drive each other crazy with their compulsive habits because they both understand the urge for perfection.

But when they interact with non-Melancholy children and friends, their perfectionism can get in the way of meaningful relationships. Instead of feeling loved and accepted for who they are, the children of a Melancholy couple often feel like they're not good enough. And the friends of a Melancholy couple will quickly grow tired of the friendship if the Melancholies don't learn to accept a little disorder. It's important for this couple to remember that being "perfect" isn't a priority for everyone.

Perfect Friends Are Hard to Find!

Unlike other couples, the double Melancholy couple never has to adjust to living with a less perfectionistic personality. Without a spouse to remind them that people are rarely perfect, both husband and wife tend to set high standards for everyone in their life.

The wife in a perfect couple once came to me and expressed a concern over their lack of friendships. I had watched her during the three days of CLASS because she had stood out as an obviously perfect personality. I had been attracted to her gorgeous clothes and sense of style. I also had watched her step back and pull herself in when people approached her at break time. It was as if to say, "Don't get too close; you might mess me up."

As I listened to this woman explain her marriage, I found out that she had been raised by a Melancholy. Her mother had raised her to be a lady. She never had play clothes as a child and was always ready in case company came. And not surprisingly, she married another Melancholy.

At church she was very involved teaching Bible studies to the women. And she had helped many of them to improve their looks and self-worth. When she hosted dinner parties, everyone came but no one would ever ask her and her husband back. They all knew it would be impossible to meet her perfect standards!

Sanguines love to visit beautiful Melancholy homes but don't plan on returning the invitation. "I'd be sure to mess everything up. I don't even have that many dishes that match. I might not set the table right." Cholerics simply don't want to spend the time to make everything as perfect as the Melancholy. They admire Melancholy perfection and would like to have them over, but they put it off until "someday when everything's perfect." Phlegmatics know they'll never invite the Melancholies over the minute they walked into the Melancholies' house. "Everything is so perfect. I could never begin to equal that. It's just too much work!"

When the other personalities fail to return a Melancholy couple's friendly invitation, the thoughtful Melancholies are hurt. And it's hard for friendship to flourish when one side feels slighted and the other feels inferior to the perfect standards of their Melancholy friends. This is not a simple problem to solve. After all, should a Melancholy have to burn the rolls to show she's human?

When the Melancholy couple comes to understand that their double strengths in detail and perfection are an intimidating standard to others, they can work to minimize this intimidation. Complimenting your friends on their own unique strengths is a great way to show that you don't look down on them for having a less-than-perfect house. Unless you are prepared to live life with few friends, you will have to learn to accept the disorder of your friends' lives without trying to "fix it" for them. And remember—they may just be able to teach you a thing or two about having fun!

Wiping the Tears Away

The Melancholy poets of old were known to weep and wail through their sadness and seek solace from another person who could commiserate with them. Melancholies will cry through a tragic movie and then talk about how sad, subtle, and sensitive the message was. "I really loved it," they'll say, even as they take

167

out another Kleenex. While those of us who are not Melancholy don't see wallowing as much fun, it is essential in the steps of Melancholy grieving.

These differences are perhaps most evident when it comes to facing the death of a loved one. Sanguines hold the funeral parties so they won't be too morbid, and they don't want to continue mourning for long. "Let's remember their happy moments and then move on. They wouldn't want us to be miserable forever." Cholerics want to clean out the closets and move on with life. To them, conversations about the deceased's life and virtues are a waste of time. And the Phlegmatics simply hide their feelings. They sense the pain but would rather not talk about it. With these typical reactions from their friends, the Melancholies have to grieve with other Melancholies or alone. They can't risk the chance of someone snapping at them, "Aren't you over it yet! Snap out of it!"

Katheryn and Harold were drawn to each other through mutual melancholia. Each was fifty and still mourning their deceased mate. They met once a week for a long breakfast and talked about how they felt with each other because no one else would listen to their pain. Even family members thought it was time to put away the hankies. What a blessing for them to be able to share their grief together!

When Katheryn and Harold began their breakfast meetings, they didn't aim to love each other but to get acquainted with each other's spouse. As Melancholies, they were willing to listen. Katheryn recalls, "I fell in love with his wife immediately. She was so fascinating to me!" Harold's wife had died ten months earlier, and he had not had anyone to talk to about her because their friends already knew everything. In his grief, he loved talking about her, and Katheryn loved hearing about her. Every time they saw each other, they cried—and enjoyed being with someone who didn't tell them to get over it.

By the time they had each relieved their process of grieving, they were able to sit back and look at each other in a new way. They learned they had the same standard in Christ. They each knew the other's deepest feelings and there was nothing to hide or suppress. They were free. With this new clarity of mind they saw the warmth, understanding, and tenderness in each other. Marriage was an obvious next step.

Since they have been married, Katheryn has shared with me how their double Melancholy grieving has affected their marriage. After learning about the personalities, they have seen that their double tendency for grief can feed off each other, causing them to constantly drop into their mutual grief. They have decided to be more positive and even develop a sense of humor.

Although they still find a lot of things to do alone, they also take breaks with friends. During the summer, Harold opens the door to his garage workshop. People passing by often stop to chat with him about what he makes, and his sense of humor comes out when they take an interest in his projects. They have also found that entertaining guests is a great way for them to enjoy a "perfect project" together while still using their sense of humor to entertain the guests.

This sense of humor has also tempered their need for perfection. When they decided to build a townhouse, they took care to ensure that all the details were done properly. But to keep their tone light, they would bring donuts and juice as "bribes" for the construction workers to do a good job on their unit.

Harold used to find such idle banter wasteful, but as he has spent hundreds of hours ministering to people in need he has seen the insatiable appetite they have for someone to care. Now he talks to every person he meets, and frequently they will pour out their problems to his listening ear. He will give them a healing plan and direct them to helpful books. Often he will take their card and mail them some material.

Both Harold and Katheryn have lightened up over the years, allowing them to spend more time enjoying the good times together rather than wallowing in the bad. They now kid around with each other that their ability to laugh at life shows that God does make all things possible.

"Stick to the Facts, Please"

Melancholy couples are real sticklers for the facts. In contrast to Sanguines, who use their charm to cover up the lack of accurate memory, the Melancholy couple considers anything one step away from the facts to be lying. Fortunately, double Melancholy couples rarely get annoyed with each other over embellished stories or stretched truths. When they see the other spending a lot of time digging for the facts, they can smile and let them continue.

Katheryn is thrilled that her Melancholy husband checks all the bills as they come in. He goes over each one meticulously, searching for errors. Harold has found in his record-keeping that 20 percent of the bills have mistakes in them. So he calls each company and helps them figure it out correctly.

While Harold works with money problems, Katheryn spends much of her time in Bible study. She uses the same detailed analysis on Scripture that he uses on money. She's not satisfied with the latest religious trend or even ideas that have circulated for centuries. Instead, she pages through concordances, investigating every concept and verse. The women in her Bible study group benefit from the surprising details Katheryn shares from her studies.

How great it is when two Melancholies can understand each other's needs to search for the facts, even when manifested in different ways. But this perfect couple will have to be careful when they're with non-Melancholy friends. They need to remember that some people enjoy the big picture more than the details. And these friends may be frustrated or offended when Melancholies interrupt their good story to correct the facts.

Learning How to Fight

Melancholy couples rarely fight—they would consider it crude or low class. Instead, they go into moods and don't tell the other why they are mad. It soon becomes a game. "If you really loved me, you'd know why I'm upset." Other Melancholies re-sort to silence and pouting to get their point across.

Beth and Jim both hate disagreeing with someone who in-sists on confronting and yelling. So when they disagree, they quickly tell each other their point of view and let each other know that they're angry with the situation. Then they go to op-posite sides of the house and sulk the rest of the day, maybe even into the next day. Eventually they get tired of it, and one of them asks, "Want to start over?" Without ever bringing the old issue up, they hug and everything is okay. Now that Jim and Beth have come to recognize what they are doing, they hug a lot sooner than they used to!

This system for dealing with conflict may be an effective way of handling some problems. Giving each other some time and space to sulk offers them a chance to "cool down" and think about things when they are in a more rational state of mind. This saves Melancholy couples from blowing up at each other and saying things they later regret. And usually, a thoughtful Melancholy will realize their selfishness and think of a good compromise that can end the sulky silence.

But sometimes this pouting can carry on for far too long. And as both sides continue the "silent treatment" toward each other, they each feel more wronged by the other. When this happens, it takes a very long time for either spouse to come back to the other so the conflict can be resolved. Sadly, some Melancholy couples miss out on a lot of enjoyment together because they spend so much time sulking over their problems instead of re-solving them.

To avoid this problem, Melancholies need to develop a sys-tem that ensures their sulking doesn't carry on for too long. If they have shared their disagreement and reached an impasse with each other, they should agree on a time when they will get back together and look at the problem again. This will allow both of them the "sulking" time that Melancholies need to think through a problem. But it will also force them to resolve the conflict before sulking becomes a permanent feature of their marriage!

Learning about the personalities can prevent the Melancholy couple from becoming an unapproachable and nit-picking pair. They will need to work on accepting the disorder of their friends and children and remember that not all pleasures in life are found in the details. But if they can learn to avoid their double weaknesses, this couple will be a pleasant pair, with friends and family who appreciate their thoughtful attention to detail.

No Time for Fun, There's Work to Be Done!—Choleric Marries Choleric

The double Choleric marriage is a work to behold. This is the marriage of achievement. Both people are goal oriented, powerful personalities who never seem to rest. They respect each other's desire, ambition, and accomplishments. They get up early, give each other their day's schedule, and march off to get the troops in order. If there was a sound track to accompany this marriage, it would include the song, "Heigh Ho! Heigh Ho! It's off to work we go!"

Choleric couples have the ability, even emotional necessity, to do more than one thing at a time. They see their time as valuable and make the most of every minute—doing only one thing at a time borders on laziness in their world. And they certainly won't waste any time on worthless projects. Their ability to multitask makes them effective leaders. This couple is praised by the church because they are consistent workers who get the job done. They run circles around others and leave observers in a state of exhaustion.

The double Choleric house is efficient, well organized, and productive. Everyone knows where they're going when, and there is no margin for error. "You know the rules!" This family turns out Choleric and Melancholy superachievers, pushes Sanguines to see beyond their desire for fun, and often gives up on motivating the Phlegmatics, thinking, "Where did we ever get him from?"

At their best, this couple will enjoy being involved in many activities together and provide reliable leadership to their friends and family. With their double strengths in motivation and completing multiple projects, they are sure to win respect and admiration for their accomplishments. And when anyone tells them, "It can't be done," the double Choleric couple will be sure to prove them wrong.

All Work, No Play

As the Sanguine is all play, the Choleric is all work. Each one has so many projects to complete that they both think of social events as a waste of time. Social life is not a high priority unless it has to do with business, and the Choleric only goes to parties if they can see some future benefit from the time wasted in idle chatter. Even vacations can turn into work sessions for the Choleric couple, and they include cell phones and briefcases as necessary items for the trip.

Fred and I are both Cholerics who love our work and have to force ourselves to set aside time for vacations. Even then, we take work along. I'm always writing a book, and he has all our planning, airlines, and finances to catch up on. Our motto is, "Don't waste your vacation on relaxation." People sometimes ask Fred and me, "When are you going to retire?" And we say, "Why? What would we rather do? We live on a golf course but we have no time for golf. We're right next to the pool, but lying around the pool is nonproductive." As our daughter Lauren once said, "If I ever wanted to rest, I sure wouldn't come home!"

The Choleric couple may be stunned when people call them busy. After all, they say, "Who else is going to get this done?" Unfortunately, this drive for work can cut out any special time for the couple to enjoy each other's company. In the midst of their projects and acitivies, they may find themselves married to a stranger. It's important for the Choleric couple to recognize that relaxation is not laziness, and every marriage needs a good dose of both from time to time.

Because Fred and I have the same Choleric core, we understand our love for work and our disdain for laziness. We also know that this diligent strength carried to an extreme can be a weakness. We can become workaholics with no friends. One of the provisions we've made to prevent this is that we don't work on airplanes. We are constantly in the air, and we've found that we need that time on each end of the trip to rest. I bring women's magazines that I don't allow myself to read at home. Both of us do crossword puzzles, and we discuss our future trips as Fred looks through travel magazines. This has become an important time for us as a couple because we give ourselves permission to relax.

Who's in Charge Here?

It's not surprising to see Choleric couples take charge and lead a group quickly to their goal. In fact, most Cholerics only want to be involved in groups where they are in charge. "If we can't be president and vice president, it's not worth our time to join."

This highly productive couple makes consistent progress as long as they are both marching in the same direction, leading the troops to victory. The problems come when they don't agree on goals, try to control each other, and undermine the other's opinion with others. "I don't care what *she* said. Listen to me!" They each need credit for all the great works they have completed, and they get upset if their mate takes credit that is rightfully theirs.

Because Cholerics blow up easily over anything that doesn't go their way, it is essential that they understand the personalities if they wish to maintain a positive relationship. Their tendency is to marry a Phlegmatic and let them know who's boss right from the beginning. But when they marry another Choleric, this is a more difficult combination because each was born to be boss. It's like a ship with two captains or a country with two presidents.

To avoid blowing up over differences, the Choleric couple should divide responsibilities so they are not both doing the same chore. Without a compromise, their mutual desire to be in charge will lead to angry outbursts, refusal to help each other, and a desire to outsmart the other one, especially in front of friends. Any of these actions will cause their mate to hate them, at least for the moment, and a repeat of these behaviors will lead to fights or plots of revenge. Neither of these responses leads to romance or even toleration.

But when they both understand that they were born with a controlling nature, they can learn to march together on the same road. When Fred and I married, we both expected to be in control of everything and frequently ignored each other's efforts to lead. Then we went through the birth and death of two brain-damaged sons and realized we were totally out of control. In our depression we went in different directions, trying to find something we could control. What we found was twofold: First, we both found the Lord, and second, we found a book explaining the personalities. We saw ourselves, as we truly were, and both our strengths and weaknesses. We were both depressed, but because of our Choleric ability to pick up the broken pieces and move on, we both studied and put our marriage back together. Within a short time we were teaching personality marriage classes in our home. In these groups we saw changed attitudes and renewed commitments as we all grew together.

175

One of the major changes we had at that time was our division of who was in charge of what. We had always overlapped our responsibilities and each tried to do things our way. So instead we started to make a list of all the things that needed to be done in the house, yard, and at work. I chose what I liked, Fred took his pick, and we split the leftovers. We made charts for the children's duties too, and put up a new one each Thursday so they would know what was expected of them for the weekend. It was not easy for me to get a new chart up every Thursday, but when I saw how the charts saved me work and got the children to do their chores without my nagging, I was more than willing to do it.

Through the years we have changed and updated our charts and had to revise our responsibilities. Fred now handles our schedules, air flights, finances, contracts, and subjects, while I get ready on time, bring the right props for the subjects, and do the majority of the speaking. In the home Fred has taken on new duties to free me up more for study and writing. He plans the menus ahead, does the marketing, cooks all the meals, and calls me when they're ready. I set the table and do the dishes.

Our life may not be like yours, but the principles are the same. Wherever you are in your progress through life, sit down, list your responsibilities, and decide who does what. Then, let each other do it—and don't hover around to make sure your spouse is doing them right! Thank each other frequently and realize that two Cholerics can have the most exciting life of any combination when you're both on the same team and marching in the same direction.

When It's Time to Let Go . . .

One couple we know well has come up with some double Choleric solutions. It is a second marriage and we knew the man in his first. He was manipulative and controlling and had temper tantrums in public places when he didn't get his way. Because he is a well-known public political figure, people learned to do things his way and avoid upsetting him. His wife finally got sick of his games and filed for divorce.

His new wife is a charming Choleric who knows how to bring out his strengths and protect him from his own weaknesses. One night we went out to dinner with them, and the maître d' had no record of our reservations. We cringed because we knew what his reaction would be. "Do you know who I am . . ." he began to say.

But his wife pushed him aside gently, stepped in front of him, and said sweetly, "I'll take care of this for you." Much to our amazement, he turned away quietly and walked over to the decorative fish tank to watch the varied specimens swim by. His wife charmed the maître d' into creating a special place just for us.

Later, I asked her about this incident, and she explained, "When he asked me to marry him, I first said no. Since there were lines of women who would have said yes, he was surprised. As he continued the pursuit, I explained the personalities and told him I would not tolerate his flare-ups. I showed him how he brought negative attention to himself that instilled fear and not admiration."

She then explained how they had made a deal. When he would feel his anger rising, he would step aside and let her take charge. If she felt he was heading for trouble, she had only to tap him and say, "I'll handle this," and he would go watch the goldfish.

What a change in a volatile man when he could see his weaknesses and was willing to do something about it! He learned the important lessons for all Cholerics to remember—that sometimes, you just have to let go and let someone else take control. These two Cholerics have taken their mutual aggressive personalities and made a dynamic team who now draws admiration instead of fear.

Forget the Fine Print

One of the areas Cholerics always share is their dislike for instructions or even road maps. Consulting infers lack of intelligence. It's better to guess than ask someone who probably won't know anyway. Reading fine print and double-checking does not appeal to the Choleric.

But this tendency can get them in trouble. My friend Bonny recently shared how her husband's failure to read instructions got their Choleric marriage into trouble. Now they are in the middle of a legal mess that is partly due to their failure to read the small print. Each one blames the other.

Cholerics' disdain for details also comes into play when it comes to learning and discussing the personalities. Like any couple, it's important for Cholerics to work on their strengths and weaknesses so they can avoid potential conflicts. But Cholerics find discussion groups to be nothing more than pooled ignorance. And when it comes to discussing their marriage relationship together, these two will quickly say, "We don't have time for that!"

The Cholerics are the least apt to sit down and talk over potential problems, because they each assume everything would be fine if only the other person would do it their way. Each tends to push the other down, wipe out their feisty spirit, and turn them into a phony Phlegmatic. Cholerics have the ability to play any role needed to achieve a goal, but suppressed Cholerics ultimately either blow up and walk out or develop psychosomatic pathology. Their mate won't accept this illness and usually suggests, "It's all in your head. Snap out of it."

Since both of these patterns diminish any desire for romance, they lead to a cold, distant marriage or a life of emotional separation. Considering these unpleasant possibilities, it is well worth the couples' time to take the personality test and talk it over while they still like each other!

In learning together about the personalities it is important to listen to each other's complaints without interruption or defensiveness, two of the worst traits of the Choleric. When one interrupts, the other fights or quits, and the conversation has a quick death. But when one keeps defending himself and won't admit any part of the blame, the other gives up. "What's the use?"

If Cholerics truly want to work on strengthening their weaknesses, they have to be honest with each other. This includes sharing what habits or sharp responses are annoying and will cause friction in the marriage. Having these discussions may be frustrating for the time-conscious Cholerics, but a balanced marriage is worth the effort.

We All Need Friends!

Cholerics need to force themselves to keep friendships and have social relationships. Their tendency is to spend time with people for business purposes, so they don't have a need for parties when they are at home. But this isolation can become a weakness when a couple's constant activity gets in the way of developing relationships.

Fred and I have learned to set aside fun times for friends. From Thanksgiving through New Year's, we don't travel on business. Instead, we accept holiday invitations and entertain many guests. Fred has taken the fun so seriously that he is often inviting people he meets traveling to come and vacation with us. Many of them do. And during these holiday parties, he almost becomes a Sanguine!

Jill and Chet have the same personality combinations as Fred and I. She's Choleric/Sanguine and he's Choleric/Melancholy. They both love their work, he as the owner and president of a business and she as a teacher and author. There are no dull moments in their lives. Because they understand their tendencies to put work above all else, they have each looked for ways to broaden their activities. To take his focus off total absorption on work, Jill suggested he could help at the church. As soon as he let his availability be known, he was put on the Board of Elders and made chairman.

Their church has two thousand members, with fifty foreign missionaries and eight daughter churches. The pastor was soon impressed by Chet's ability to get an overview of the situation, organize, and delegate. Two months into the chairmanship, he had everything so well put together that he could truly enjoy himself, share jokes with the other men, and even relax. Prior to this church committee, Chet had no friends beyond the acquaintances he made in his business. Now Jill is delighted to see him developing friendships that will last forever.

Jill herself tries to make sure that part of her Choleric energy is channeled into developing and keeping friends. Using her Choleric strengths in planning and motivating, she has been able to stay in contact with many old friends for years. Within her busy schedule of teaching, writing, and organizing family events, she continues to make time for relationships with her family and friends because she is more flexible.

Thankfully, both Jill and Chet have learned to spread themselves out beyond their work and to build some lasting friendships. If Choleric couples don't make this a priority, they ultimately find themselves retired, with no work and no friends who really care.

The Choleric couple needs to work on dividing their responsibilities, taking time to discuss their personalities, and taking the time for vacations and friends. When this busy couple recognizes the value of rest and rejuvenation, they will find that they have even more energy and zest for life. But more importantly, they will enjoy the blessing of deep friendships and a balanced marriage.

Don't Look Lazy; It'll Drive Others Crazy—Phlegmatic Marries Phlegmatic

The double Phlegmatic combination creates a very relaxed marriage. They have one of the most peaceful and agreeable relationships imaginable, and rare is the moment when two Phlegmatics confront each other over anything. Nothing is worth a fight to this peaceful duo. And nothing is worth the effort either. For Phlegmatics, working all day is enough—when they come home from work, they are ready to relax.

Two Phlegmatics get along with everyone, have no enemies, and are socially unpretentious. They are genuine friends and do nothing for show. When it comes to children, Phlegmatic parents are a very patient pair who don't put too much pressure on their kids. Their relaxed attitude is sure to keep peace in the home.

When it comes to projects, the Phlegmatics simply say, "What projects?" Planning ahead is just too much effort for them. They are content with what they have and rarely take on big home improvement projects. It's hard to find fault with Phlegmatics, unless you are the Choleric mother-in-law who can't believe they haven't done a thing with their place since the last time she was there!

But this peaceful, stable pair can fall into a dull rut if they don't work to prevent their double weaknesses from taking over the marriage. Without some effort, their fear of conflict will prevent them from enjoying genuine communication with each other. And their easygoing parenting style allows children to take over the home.

At their best, however, this quiet couple works to take control of their children and their home. Being satisfied with a modest home, they will not fall into the hectic and hurried pace of those around them. Instead, this agreeable pair will enjoy many fun and peaceful moments with their family, friends, and each other.

"Let's Just Do It Later"

As the Sanguine only wants to do something if it's fun, the Choleric only wants to do something if they are in charge, and the Melancholy only wants to do something if they can do it perfectly—the Phlegmatic just doesn't want to do it!

Avoiding pledges of commitment is a unique Phlegmatic talent. They will nod and stall until someone else does the task for them. So what happens when two Phlegmatics are married to each other? Nothing much!

Imagine two Phlegmatics discussing household chores:

Phlegmatic #1: "The garage needs a good cleaning."
Phlegmatic #2: "I hadn't noticed."
Phlegmatic #1: "Saturday might be a good time to do it."

Phlegmatic #2: "Fine, if you feel like it."

Phlegmatic #1: "Well, I'll only do it if you'll help."

Phlegmatic #2: "Then you can forget it."

Phlegmatic #1: "As long as we can get the car in, I guess it's okay."

Phlegmatic #2: "It's okay with me."

In contrast to the Choleric/Phlegmatic marriage where the Phlegmatic has to look busy in order to stay out of trouble, the double Phlegmatic marriage is the big easy. They're not in a hurry to get things done and will easily agree to delay the household chores—"It doesn't matter. It'll still be there tomorrow."

Their aim is to avoid conflict, do it the easiest way, and live in peace. They have learned that half the things people worry about never end up happening. They know that if they do or don't show up at church, no one notices, and if they don't go to the meetings, they won't be elected president or have to do any work. Much of their limited energy is spent on figuring out how not to spend the rest of the energy that's left over. They should win an award for energy conservation!

Living Room Turned into a Closet

Interior decorating is a foreign thought to two Phlegmatics. The Sanguine relocates chairs, nails up new pictures, and drapes bright fabric over anything that doesn't move (including Phlegmatic children). The Choleric is always open for new ideas that will make the house more functional, more washable, or money saving. And the Melancholy wants to study home and garden magazines, compare prices, and wait until they have enough money to decorate perfectly. The Phlegmatics see no reason in changing anything at all. "We're used to it this way."

One Phlegmatic couple I know bought a furnished model home in a development. They have lived there ten years and haven't changed a thing. "If it looked good in the beginning, there's no need to change it now." Some other Phlegmatic friends bought a house with a formal living room and a casual family room. They put old furniture in the family room and left the living room empty until they had time to go shopping or an inclination to decorate. It's been seven years now, and the room has become a large storage closet—but they really don't care!

While their easygoing attitude does save them from the hectic or detailed projects of other couples, sometimes this attitude can become a problem. A double Phlegmatic couple has to work on completing basic household chores. If they don't, their non-Phlegmatic children and friends are sure to be frustrated by the constant sloppiness of the home. And they also need to remember that some projects only become worse when they are put off. For the safety of their home and family, they need to make an effort to repair damages before they get worse.

What Goals?

Just as Phlegmatics avoid work and projects, they avoid planning ahead. As long as they can relax and enjoy themselves, they see no need to set goals or make plans for the future.

Paula is a Choleric who makes major decisions in a split second and works efficiently as an executive assistant and head of her home. Her Phlegmatic son Jim is a very intelligent boy and is also her complete opposite. Paula had lofty ambitions for Jim, but he didn't want to follow her plan. He just liked to drive. When Paula would ask, "Where are you going?" he would shrug and say, "I don't know. Wherever the car takes me, I guess."

"How could you go just anywhere without a goal?" Paula would ask. He'd shrug again and leave.

Those of you Cholerics can imagine the frustration when her son chose to skip college and go to truck-driving school. "What is truck-driving school?" she asked.

183

"It's where you go to get a license to drive trucks as a profession," Jim responded.

"A profession? Driving trucks?" Paula was disappointed with Jim's decision, not because she didn't like truck drivers but because she knew his bright mind was capable of so much more. She hoped he would marry a girl who could motivate him toward using some of his unique gifts.

Instead, he met a Phlegmatic who shared his lack of interest in long-term goals. Jim has now been happily driving trucks for ten years. "It's so peaceful. You just relax and listen to music all day."

Had Jim and his girlfriend learned about the personalities, they might have been able to see that their double Phlegmatic relationship was not encouraging either of them to develop their talents. Phlegmatic couples need to work on setting at least a few long-term goals. If they do not deliberately make some plans, they are not likely to use their God-given abilities to accomplish anything.

What's the Hurry?

Phlegmatics are never in a hurry to get anything done. If it takes them a long time to do daily chores, it takes even longer for them to make lifestyle changes or decisions.

It was on one of Jim's truck-driving trips that he met Judy, a nice, quiet Phlegmatic girl. True to their Phlegmatic natures, they were in no hurry to get married. They dated steadily for several years and talked about a wedding "someday." But the work of purchasing a ring and planning a wedding just seemed like too much effort for this pair. Their friends and family were perplexed by the two—for all their talk of getting married, they were taking a very long time to get engaged.

It was not in Judy's Phlegmatic nature to spend a long time shopping around for a wedding dress. One day, she saw a sale on wedding gowns and decided to buy one for the future. It was a convenient time for her and would save her having to make the effort after she and Jim were engaged.

Fortunately, Jim found a ring at a discount that happened to fit her. Otherwise this Phlegmatic couple might never have gotten engaged! He bought it as a sign of commitment and his Choleric mother, Paula, finally rejoiced that the wedding plans could begin.

In their quiet Phlegmatic way, both Jim and Judy sat back while their families talked about and began planning the wedding. They actually preferred it that way. After all, these two Phlegmatics disliked planning ahead or doing anything that required a lot of effort. They were content to be engaged and were in no hurry to have a fancy wedding and go through the work of setting up a home. After some time, even Paula began to lose hope that these two would ever walk down the aisle.

In the end, Judy had the gown in the closet for five years and the ring on her finger for four when they finally decided to get married. By that time, their families had lost all enthusiasm for the wedding. They were just happy to see them finally married!

Like Jim and Judy, many Phlegmatic couples are content to sit, wait, and let others do their work for them. Obviously, this becomes a problem in a Phlegmatic marriage when neither spouse steps in to take control and get things done. And when there are strong-willed children in the home, they tend to push aside their Phlegmatic parents and take control themselves.

Phlegmatic couples should make sure that they don't keep putting off major life decisions until "a better time." They might miss out on some wonderful opportunities or allow themselves to be taken over by controlling children who make decisions for them.

"You Decide"

Because Phlegmatics hate conflict, they are always trying to keep the peace. They often defer the decision-making to someone else because they are afraid of choosing something that the other person won't like. Besides, contented Phlegmatics really don't care what decisions are made anyway.

When Jim and Judy finally did get married, they got a little apartment and settled in. One day Paula was going to be in their area, and she called to say she'd pick up a pizza and bring it over for a supper together. She had a spare hour and some half-price pizza coupons and would love to see them.

"What kind of pizza would you like?" she asked. This seemed like a simple question, but they had to discuss it.

In typical Phlegmatic fashion, the couple avoided making the decision. "Why don't you just come over, and we'll decide by the time you get here," they said, hoping Jim's mom would just make the decision herself.

When Paula arrived, Judy and Jim were still scrambling to scrub the kitchen floor and vacuum the messy living room. By the time they pulled themselves together, it was too late for them to eat together, so Jim's mom gave them money and the coupons, told them to have a pleasant time, and left. Jim and Judy still refer to that evening as one of the nicest times they'd ever had. Paula just shakes her Choleric head in disbelief.

Buried Conflicts

The Phelgmatic couple always appears peaceful and relaxed to their family and friends. This duo also keeps their happy faces on for each other. Peaceloving Phlegmatics just want to avoid conflict or disagreement at all costs, so they will pretend to be content with each other even when they are silently upset.

But when Phlegmatics put all their effort into avoiding any discussion of a problem, they never actually solve it. Instead, both spouses repress the hurt and live with underlying anger or pain that needs to be discussed. When a Phlegmatic is married to a non-Phlegmatic, the non-Phlegmatic can be the one to initiate discussions about difficult topics. But when Phlegmatics are married to each other, neither one wants to raise disagreeable issues, and their feelings are never discussed.

It's not difficult to see that the Phlegmatic couple's avoidance of conflict can soon lead to a lack of meaningful communication. For all their agreeable conversations, they will never challenge each other to grow or share their deep concerns about marriage and life. This couple may need to write down their concerns ahead of time and then pick a time to share them with each other each week, no matter how uncomfortable it makes them. But their effort will be well worth it as they realize the joy and satisfaction of triumphing over their problems together.

Phlegmatic couples will benefit greatly as they learn to understand the strengths and weaknesses of their personality. With both spouses committed to having a great marriage, they can put in the effort that is needed to keep their home in repair, their children under control, and their communication lines open. And with both eyes open to their weaknesses, this couple will enjoy a stable and satisfying lifetime together.

ten

CREATING YOUR OWN UNIQUE SONG

A Few Notes for All Couples

Now that you have seen how different personality combinations work together, you and your spouse can enjoy your own special blend. As you recognize your similarities and differences, you know that God's desire for your marriage is that you compromise, integrate, and meet each other's needs.

In this chapter, you can take a last look at the four personalities in marriage. The bits of advice found here will be a benefit for any couple who wants to strengthen their marriage. No matter what your combination of personalities is, these concepts will help you and your spouse stay in tune.

Communicating Needs

Seldom do we think of communicating our emotional needs, and yet these unmet needs cause disharmony in marriage. Just picture the following combination and you begin to see why differing needs cause hot conflict. The talkative Sanguine, who wants constant attention and approval for every little thing they do, marries a Melancholy, who is looking for support but won't ask for it and enjoys silence. The Melancholy won't approve of the Sanguine because nothing they do is perfect, and the Melancholy can't stand the Sanguine's babbling and need for attention. But the Sanguine can't function without praise, even if it's undeserved, and they can't stand someone who won't tell them what's the matter. When neither one gets what they need on an emotional level, they pull away and often look for someone else to fill their needs.

In a Choleric/Phlegmatic marriage, the Choleric needs appreciation for all the work they do, but a Phlegmatic mate won't be manipulated into praise. A Phlegmatic's response to the Choleric's accomplishment will more than likely be, "I didn't ask you to do it" or "It was your idea." The Choleric works constantly and can't understand why the Phlegmatic doesn't get excited over one more new project. The Phlegmatic wants emotional peace and learns to tune out on the Choleric's frenzy. Phlegmatics wish to be accepted and loved the way they are, but Cholerics naturally feel that they need to continue "training" their spouse.

Even couples who share the same personality can sometimes find themselves frustrated at trying to fill each other's emotional needs. Though they may be quicker to understand each other's needs than other couples, they are still individuals with their own perspectives and concerns.

No personality theory can give you a perfect key for unlocking every mystery in your spouse. Learning about the personalities is a great benefit to your marriage—but it cannot be a substitute for good communication between you and your spouse.

When you begin to feel that your needs are going unmet, don't keep your spouse guessing about what's wrong. Remember, they have their own unique personality and that makes it difficult for them to see things from your perspective.

Instead, take the time to sit down with each other and talk about your needs. You may be surprised to learn that the things you thought your spouse would appreciate the most are the very things that annoy them to no end! Clearly communicating your needs helps your spouse understand how to show you love in a way that you will appreciate. And once you begin feeling loved, you can't help but reciprocate, starting a healthy cycle of love that keeps drawing you and your spouse together.

Table for Two

Marriage often becomes a victim of the busy world around us. Balancing work, friends, family, and social activities is a challenge for most couples. Amidst deadlines, crying children, and daily chores, most couples have little or no time for meaningful communication. The days of dating and romance fade fast once that wedding ceremony is over! But it doesn't have to be that way.

Joyce and Steve have been married thirty years and have achieved a balance that serves as a beautiful example of the personalities at their best. Joyce is a motivated Phlegmatic who is willing to spend hours listening to women's problems and leading them into solutions. Steve is a Choleric businessman who is focused on his work but has learned to put that aside when he comes home. They understand their differences and work to keep them from conflicting.

During the week Joyce has time for friends and relatives, for attending conferences, and for the shopping she enjoys. Her children are grown, and she is enjoying her much-deserved freedom. But on the weekends Joyce and Steve only make plans that include them both. As Joyce explained to me, "When we are together we really are together. We like it that way!"

So what has been the secret of their success?

One way that Joyce and Steve have worked to keep their personalities in harmony is by setting aside special times for each other. Besides being close companions, sharing the family, and being intimate with one another, they have dates at regular times during the week. They go to a restaurant and focus on each other and what's going on in each other's lives. Now that they have more resources and their children are no longer under-foot, Joyce and Steve have been able to take longer trips alone as well.

Setting aside these special times together has kept the spark in their marriage for thirty years. As they have taken time to recognize each other's personality traits, they have been able to resolve conflicts and stay in love. In a letter about her marriage, Joyce writes, "We are soul mates and true lovers after all these years. I am the grace to his works."

If you are looking for a way to keep the communication lines open in your marriage, you have to start by making time to communicate. Carve out time from your schedule to spend alone and without interruptions. In moments away from the hectic activities of daily life, you and your spouse can enjoy each other's company and take time to discuss what has been going on in both of your lives. For most of us, though, these special moments alone will need to be planned if they are going to happen at all. So take out the calendar, set aside some time, and make some reservations for a table for two!

Retirement Games

"If you thought marriage was difficult in normal times, wait until you retire."

This is a comment I overheard while at a women's retreat for seniors. Instead of feeling freedom in retirement, this woman felt panic.

Rosalie had these same feelings when her husband retired. Rosalie has an "opposites attract" marriage. Rosalie is a typical Choleric; she likes to take charge of situations and speak her mind without batting an eye. Her husband, Stan, is the Plegmatic type. He's easygoing and will do almost anything to avoid conflict. But the personality strengths that charmed and attracted them at first turned into major irritations for Rosalie when Stan retired. Their togetherness twenty-four hours a day, seven days a week, became a real challenge.

Rosalie says, "When my husband neared retirement, I dreamed of the utopian life—traveling to exciting places, pursuing hobbies, and relaxing on the porch swing together. With the nest empty, I was ready for fun and games. However, some of the games I never envisioned us playing were the thermostat relay and supermarket hide-and-seek."

After going through menopause and gaining twenty pounds, Rosalie always felt hot. During the summer she grumbled about the heat and humidity, then rushed to the thermostat to turn the air conditioning up. But Stan had a circulation problem. His legs and feet were always cold, even in a summer heat wave. Unlike Rosalie, Stan preferred the silent approach to problem solving. He would wait patiently until Rosalie had gone out of the room, then turn the air conditioning off. In the winter, their goals were reversed: He would turn the heat up, and she would go behind him and turn it down. Like a yo-yo their thermostat went up and down as they played thermostat relay every day.

Another game Rosalie and Stan would play is supermarket hide-and-seek. As an organized Choleric, Rosalie went about shopping in a very businesslike way. She carried a list, operated on a time schedule, and stayed within a specific budget. She felt that shopping with another person was a burden that dragged her down. When Stan retired, however, she could no longer enjoy the luxury of shopping alone because Stan often joined her as she did the weekly grocery shopping. When she wasn't looking, he would take her shopping cart and sneak off with it, leaving her in the produce section with heavy bags of cantaloupes and apples. Rosalie would be forced to play hide-and-seek while lugging the bags of fruit, trying to find Stan. Meanwhile, Stan was usually throwing several boxes of his favorite cereals in the cart. The total bill would end up being twenty-five dollars over what Rosalie would normally spend.

Rosalie and Stan present us with a humorous scenario of the games we play, especially at the time of retirement. For those of you with the combination of Choleric wife and Phlegmatic husband, the following suggestions may help you all to win the games.

Phlegmatics hate dissension and would rather lie than face a real issue. "Who's angry?" they'll say. At this point, the Choleric, if not prayerfully prepared, may want to scream, but thermostat relay can't be won by fighting. There are several possible ways to to deal with this problem. You can continue to play thermostat relay by pushing the temperature up and down all day. You can come to a compromise setting and agree not to change it. Or you can have one person be in charge of the thermostat one week and the other person in charge the next. The average Phlegmatic male will choose the first option and leave well enough alone, but hopefully his Choleric wife can convince him that the other two options will work as long as neither of them cheat.

Fred and I have come up with a solution to supermarket hide-and-seek that works for us. We take two carts and go our merry ways, dividing the grocery list and each getting what we have on our paper. (If you are on a tight budget, you should agree to only get what is on the list.) Fred has a signal for when he is done with his shopping. It's a certain whistle that I'd know anywhere. One day we were separated in a mall, and we had agreed not to go farther than wing B. He met some friends, and they asked where I was. Fred said I was in one of the stores, but that he'd get me for them. He whistled, and in no time I appeared. They were impressed.

For those of you women who are not Choleric, you may think these retirement games are unusual problems. Maybe you love having your husband with you all the time, but Choleric women feel hindered, slowed down, spied on, followed, judged, and babysat. They need their space. This doesn't mean they are self-centered, only that they know the limits of their patience.

Rosalie advises, "Get him involved and then go out with a clear conscience. Being joined at the hip during all activities is hard on both parties. There is joy in a certain degree of separation. Accepting each other's differences takes an understanding of the personality types and the grace of God. How boring it would be if we all reacted the same and mirrored each other's actions. Honoring each other's uniqueness makes us emotionally and spiritually mature."

Dealing with the Down Times

The word "depression" literally means "pressed down" or not up to your usual bounce. In marriage we find it difficult to understand why the other person is depressed when we are not. Until we understand innate differences, we try to cheer the other person on by curt encouragements. "Snap out of it!" "Think of the starving children in China." Words like these put a coating of guilt on depression. Double trouble!

What we need in place of phony cheer is an understanding of our mate's sad feelings, whether or not we have ever felt the same way ourselves. We should ask, "What should I do or what should I avoid?'

Sanguine Depression

Sanguines get depressed when life is no fun or when they feel like no one appreciates them. Their thoughts tend to float down one of the following paths:

"Life is all work and no one notices how hard I try. . . ."

"Things are never going to get better and I'll never have enough money. . . ."

"Why did I ever get married? I used to be popular, and look at me now."

Sanguines get depressed in short spurts when circumstances overwhelm them. They can put on a happy face and push aside their feelings if company comes or a shopping excursion arises. Their natural response is to look for fun, eat, party, go shopping, or spend a lot of money.

When Sanguines get depressed they begin to think they are becoming a Melancholy. "My personality has changed," they say—and then that becomes another thing to be depressed about. Even though these Sanguines may exhibit a different personality while they are depressed, their basic personality doesn't change. When the hard times pass, they will be back to their sunny Sanguine self.

What to Do with a Depressed Sanguine:

- Give them "Poor babies" and be sorry. Give them gifts or cards.
- Take them out for lunch. Call more often.
- Compliment them. Let them talk it out and cry.
- Give them sincere hope that life will get better.

What to Avoid with a Depressed Sanguine:

- Don't lecture them about their failings with sayings like, "If only you had listened to me in the first place, you wouldn't be in this mess."
- Don't compare them with people worse off.
- Don't give religious clichés. "It's sin in your life." "God is trying to teach you a lesson." "God is punishing you for. . . ."
- Don't give guilt trips. They immobilize the Sanguine from any positive steps toward a solution.

195

Melancholy Depression

Melancholies get depressed when life isn't perfect, and they frequently have a feeling of impending doom. They are worn down by people who don't get serious, who don't care about details, and who don't see what their thoughtlessness is doing to the world. Because of their deep thoughtfulness and sensitivity, a Melancholy's feelings are easily hurt—and this can become another source of depression.

Their natural reaction to depression is to work even harder at getting things perfect. They will think even more than usual, analyzing a problem from every angle imaginable. Melancholies often retreat during depression, taking time to write, chart their problem out, or search for answers in a book.

Melancholies get depressed more than others because of their desire for perfection. After all, life is rarely perfect. They feel like others don't take them seriously enough. And their natural tendency toward depression causes them to miss the rainbows of life and to only see the rain.

What to Do with a Depressed Melancholy:

- Say, "I don't blame you."
- Sit quietly until they want to talk.
- Discuss possible solutions.
- Admit that life is not fair.
- Get into the pit with them and commiserate.

What to Avoid with a Depressed Melancholy:

- Don't say, "That's the stupidest thing I ever heard" or "Look at the bright side of life."
- Don't trivialize their grief and depression.
- Don't insist they cheer up today.
- Don't give up on them because that is what they expect.

Choleric Depression

Cholerics get depressed when things get out of control. They can stand just about anything as long as they can see a way to control it. If money or work will fix it, they won't fall apart because they can always work harder and earn more money.

But if it's a loss of job, money, position, or title, they will be saddened about their lack of accomplishment. If it's a diagnosis of a fatal disease or a debilitating accident, Cholerics become depressed.

A Choleric's natural reaction to depression is to work harder, exercise more, and try anything that will give them control. When life becomes out of control enough for a Choleric to drop into serious depression, suicide appears as a powerful, quick option.

What to Do with a Depressed Choleric:

- Encourage them with hope of victory.
- Tell them, "You can do it!"
- Say, "You are the smartest person I know."
- Help them come up with practical steps.

What to Avoid with a Depressed Choleric:

- Don't give out pity—it brings more depression to a Choleric.
- Don't tell them God was just trying to get their attention.
- Don't tell them their depression is caused by too much work and they should try to take it easy or go on vacation.

197

Phlegmatic Depression

Phlegmatics get depressed when the tasks ahead seem overwhelming. They start to feel down when they have to take charge. Their thoughts will start to follow this pattern: "Life is falling apart. I have to face reality. The responsibility is on me. There's nowhere

I can dump this, and it isn't fair. Why didn't somebody do something about this?"

The natural result of Phlegmatic depression is for them to pull back and isolate themselves from the problem. When a problem seems too overwhelming, they simply quit trying to solve it.

Phlegmatics don't appear to be depressed because they have learned to hide their feelings and not show they're upset. They don't complain about their depression, but they do tune out other problems and the family—they are just too overwhelmed to listen.

What to Do with a Depressed Phlegmatic:

- Agree with their assessment. "Life isn't fair." "You've been a good person." "You don't deserve this."
- Tell them you'll help them. "We'll come up with some solution."

What to Avoid with a Depressed Phlegmatic:

- Don't give Choleric commands—"Get up." "Face it." "Cheer up." "You're making a big deal out of nothing."
- Don't review your own problems and how you controlled them. Superman stories will only make the Phlegmatic feel overwhelmed by what it will take to overcome the problem.
- Don't ridicule them. Saying things to your kids about your spouse like, "Your father's a wreck again; just ignore him," will only make your spouse more depressed.

Be There

Depression does not need to be severe for it to take its toll on an individual or a marriage. If spouses aren't willing to be there for each other in the hard times, their marriage is sure to encounter some very rocky waters. But helping each other face and overcome depression can bring a couple to a deeper level of commitment.

In general, never add blame or guilt on depressed people. Even if the problem is their fault, they need to overcome their dark feelings by having some positive encouragement from their loved one. Once the dark cloud begins to lighten, you can talk about solutions and how to prevent the problem from arising again.

It is also very important to deal with a depressed person out of their personality instead of out of yours. Try to relate to them in a way that their personality will understand. Realize that this is a special time to show them that you care. It is vitally important to the health of your marriage that you be there for your spouse during their downtimes—physically, mentally, emotionally, and spiritually.

A Learning Experience

I recently spoke with a woman who had a difficult struggle with depression. As she told me her story, I was amazed at how God has used the experience to teach both her and her husband how to care for each other during their hard times.

Theresa was a bright Sanguine who loved her work and loved being around people. But after she experienced two head injuries, extreme fatigue, and illness, she began to feel depressed. Losing her job because of these disabilities brought her farther down. Life wasn't fun anymore, she didn't get to see people very often, and her natural response was to start wearing a Melancholy mask.

Her Choleric husband was very understanding throughout the entire experience, but he soon became depressed himself. Prior to Theresa's health problems, they had always been on the giving end of life—very involved with church activities and programs that helped others. But with Theresa's depression and her loss of income for three years, he felt like life had gotten out of control. Suddenly they were the ones asking for help to pay the gas bill and receiving assistance from the Salvation Army. Theresa's husband kept trying to solve their financial problems, rising at 4:45 each morning to do extra work. But it never seemed

199

to be enough, and he continued to feel that life was beyond his control.

It was during this difficult time of life that Theresa and her husband learned about the personalities. Using the principles of the personalities, they could understand and cope with things that came their way and overcome them instead of blaming each other. They also came to understand the unique reasons for their depression and what they could do to lift each other up.

Through the experience, Theresa explained, they have both learned a great deal. God has used the experience to teach them how to be on the receiving end of charity without feeling humiliated. And while many other couples would have called it quits due to the stress of her illness, God brought them closer together through the hard times.

There has been no quick fix for Theresa and her husband, but they are slowly regaining some financial ground. They have kept relationships with friends without complaining, and Theresa now lifts others up with her optimism. The joy of the Lord has truly become their strength.

When It's Time to Ask for Help

Sometimes couples reach a point in their marriage when they feel like there is no more hope. They don't love each other anymore. They are constantly annoyed by each other. They fight all the time. And they feel like there is no way to restore the special attraction that once held them together. It is at times like these that a couple needs to ask for outside help.

Sadly, many of these couples will simply adjust to a loveless marriage and go through the rest of life as two individuals united only in name. Others will file for divorce and hope for a better outcome with someone else. Often, these decisions are made before a couple has really exhausted all attempts to revive their marriage. They are embarrassed to ask for help, so they call it quits.

If you and your spouse feel like you have reached a dead end in your marriage, don't give up. Seek out the advice of godly family and friends and schedule some time to talk with a pastor or counselor.

Fred and I are grateful for the large number of counselors and pastors who use our Personality Profile in helping their clients understand their strengths and weaknesses. They tell us it is such a simple way to help people see why they don't get along with their mates. Many couples have had new life breathed into their marriage by taking the time to talk through their differences with a counselor. Counselors are trained to guide people through their discussions in a way that will bring them closer together rather than tearing them farther apart. And the time and effort spent on trying to save their marriage will teach them a lot about themselves—it is never wasted time!

The Best of Times—The Worst of Times

When spouses come to truly understand each other's personalities, they can make the best of their unique blend. Their marriage will provide true joy in the good times and true comfort through the hard times. The following story provides a fitting end to our discussion of the personalities because it shows us how a marriage built on mutual understanding can survive both the good times and the bad.

In the summer of 1985, Betsy and Rod found themselves at a new point in their marriage. They were the proud parents of a new baby boy, even though doctors had earlier told them they would never be able to have children. Betsy had recently resigned from the nursing job she'd held for eight years, and Rod had just finished his residency in radiation oncology. He made the transition to being a staff physician at Kaiser Permanente in Hollywood, California. And when their baby, Andrew, was six weeks old, they moved to Glendale, California.

201

As a very strong Sanguine/Choleric, Betsy had a difficult time making the transition to stay-at-home mom. With postpartum depression on top of all the other changes in her life, her Sanguine spirit was in desperate need of some attention, affection, and appreciation. She felt isolated in their new home and was frustrated that life seemed beyond her control, and these factors simply magnified her depressed feelings. Melancholy/Phlegmatic Rod, by contrast, needed a lot of peace, quiet, and space to just relax after a hard day's work. In a new home, working a new job, fathering a new baby, and seeing a completely different wife, his Phlegmatic nature was feeling overwhelmed, and he was looking for emotional support. Not surprisingly, both of them began to feel that their emotional needs were not being met.

And so the cycle started, the vacuum of unmet emotional needs that sucks a couple into a whirlwind of desperation. Rod would leave early every morning, and then it was just Betsy and baby Andrew. She loved being with Andrew, but she also needed someone to talk to and pay attention to her. So the minute Rod came through the door, she would say, "Talk to me, Rod. Please pay attention to me! Do you love me?" Then the Choleric side of Betsy would kick in, and she'd start telling him to study for some upcoming tests. As he would walk away to do that, her Sanguine side would pop back up and feel abandoned and unloved.

Then Rod, being true to his personality, would try to control the situation by saying nothing—one of the worst things a person can do to a needy Sanguine. This would arouse the Choleric side of Betsy, and her consuming project would be to make him talk to her. But these actions would just push Rod farther away. In his quiet Phlegmatic way, Rod would just try to avoid the conflict by taking Andrew out alone on long walks or playing long hours of video games. This cycle was killing their marriage, and both of them were feeling emotionally dry.

Over time, Betsy found that she could have her emotional needs met by getting involved at church. She received lots of positive affirmation for her work, and she felt like she was in control over this area of her life. Rod couldn't quite figure out why she felt the need to be so heavily involved, but it did seem to make her happy, so he didn't object. But even as they settled into a somewhat more balanced pattern, there continued to be an undercurrent of emotional conflict that drifted in and out of their marriage.

When Andrew was about four years old, Betsy's sister loaned them a copy of the *Personality Plus* cassette tapes. As they listened to the explanation of the personalities, they began to change their perspective and expectations of each other. It was the start of a chain of events that led them to begin accepting each other for who God made them to be.

Betsy now gives Rod the space he needs and lets him know that he has her deepest support and respect. And Rod now knows how important it is to keep encouraging and affirming Betsy in all that she does. As Betsy finished sharing her story with me, she said, "It's been sixteen years now, and God took an emotionally bankrupt marriage and turned it into an investment with rich returns."

Thank God for blessing us all with the tools to turn our marriages around. Like Betsy and Rod, we can appreciate our spouse's special personality and accept the person God created him or her to be. With our spouse we can create a beautiful song that keeps playing through sunshine or rain and turns our worst times into the best of times.

CONCLUSION

. . . And They Lived Happily Ever After

Remember the beginning of the book when I explained that most fairy tales end with a wedding? Now that you and your spouse understand the personalities, you have what it takes to figure out the rest of the story. Instead of simply wondering what it would take for you to live happily ever after together, you can get to work on creating your own fairy tale.

By now you should have an understanding of what can go on behind the curtains in every loving relationship. A good marriage starts with the auditions, continues through rehearsals and daily performances, and depends on the cast and crew working together under a faithful director—God. This all requires a lot of commitment and work—after all, we can't change our ways overnight. But I hope you and your spouse will find it worthwhile to use the Personality principles.

As you begin to understand yourself and your mate, you will learn how to work together with wisdom and knowledge. Soon you and your spouse will be performing your own special routine, winning rave reviews, and making both of your personalities shine. Just don't be surprised when others start asking you the secret to living happily ever after!

A TIMELINE OF PERSONALITY DISCOVERIES

300 B.C.	Hippocrates develops theory of inherited temperament traits
149 A.D.	Roman physiologist, Galen, proposes theory of personalities caused by levels of bodily fluids
1866	Genes discovered
1871	DNA and other nucleic acids discovered
1951	Insulin and other proteins sequenced
1953	Structure of DNA discovered
1960	New understanding of genetic code
1975–79	First human genes located
1977	DNA sequencing begins
1986	DNA sequencing first automated
1989	First disease gene located: cystic fibrosis
1995	First genome sequenced: meningitis
1999	First human chromosome sequenced
	Human genome map completed
	Working drafts first published.

Gannett News Service Research, February 12, 2001

AN OVERVIEW OF THE PERSONALITIES

POPULAR SANGUINES
"LET'S DO IT THE FUN WAY."

Desire:	have fun
Emotional needs:	attention, approval, affection, acceptance, presence of people and activity
Key strengths:	ability to talk about anything at any time at any place, bubbling personality, optimism, sense of humor, storytelling ability, enjoyment of people
Key weaknesses:	disorganized, can't remember details or names, exaggerates, not serious about anything, trust others to do the work, too gullible and naïve
Get depressed when:	life is no fun and no one seems to love them
Are afraid of:	being unpopular or bored, having to live by the clock, having to keep a record of money spent
Like people who:	listen and laugh, praise and approve

Dislike people who: criticize, don't respond to their humor, don't think they are cute

Are valuable in work for: colorful creativity, optimism, light touch, cheering up others, entertaining

Could improve if they: got organized, didn't talk so much, learned to tell time

As leaders they: excite, persuade, and inspire others; exude charm and entertain; are forgetful and poor on follow-through

Reaction to stress: leave the scene, go shopping, find a fun group, create excuses, blame others

Recognized by their: constant talking, loud volume, bright eyes

POWERFUL CHOLERICS
"LET'S DO IT MY WAY."

Desire: have control

Emotional needs: appreciation for all achievements, opportunity for leadership, participation in family decisions, something to control

Key strengths: ability to take charge of anything instantly and to make quick, correct judgments

Key weaknesses: too bossy, domineering, autocratic, insensitive, impatient, unwilling to delegate or give credit to others

Get depressed when: life is out of control and people won't do things their way

Are afraid of: losing control of anything

Like people who: are supportive and submissive, see things their way, cooperate quickly, let them take credit

Dislike people who: are lazy and not interested in working constantly, buck their authority, become independent, aren't loyal

Are valuable in work because they: can accomplish more than anyone else in a shorter time, are usually right

Could improve if they: allowed others to make decisions, delegated authority, became more patient, didn't expect everyone to produce as they do

As leaders they have:	a natural feel for being in charge, a quick sense of what will work, a sincere belief in their ability to achieve, a potential to over-whelm less aggressive people
Reaction to stress:	tighten control, work harder, exercise more, get rid of the offender
Recognized by their:	fast-moving approach, quick grab for control, self-confidence, restless and overpowering attitude

PERFECT MELANCHOLIES
"LET'S DO IT THE RIGHT WAY."

Desire:	have it right
Emotional needs:	sense of stability, space, silence, sensitivity, support
Key strengths:	ability to organize and set long-range goals, have high standards and ideals, analyze deeply
Key weaknesses:	easily depressed, spend too much time on preparation, too focused on details, remember negatives, suspicious of others
Get depressed when:	life is out of order, standards aren't met, and no one seems to care
Are afraid of:	no one understanding how they really feel, making a mistake, having to compromise standards
Like people who:	are serious, intellectual, deep, and will carry on a sensible conversation
Dislike people who:	are lightweights, forgetful, late, disorganized, superficial, prevaricating, and unpredictable
Are valuable in work for:	sense of detail, love of analysis, follow-through, high standards of performance, compassion for the hurting
Could improve if they:	didn't take life quite so seriously, didn't insist others be perfectionists
As leaders they:	organize well, are sensitive to people's feelings, have deep creativity, want quality performance
Reaction to stress:	withdraw, get lost in a book, become depressed, give up, recount the problems

Recognized by their: serious and sensitive nature, well-mannered approach, self-deprecating comments, meticulous and well-groomed looks

PEACEFUL PHLEGMATIC
"LET'S DO IT THE EASY WAY."

Desire: avoid conflict, keep peace

Emotional needs: peace and relaxation, attention, praise, self-worth, loving motivation

Key strengths: balance, even disposition, dry sense of humor, pleasing personality

Key weaknesses: lack of decisiveness, enthusiasm, and energy, a hidden will of iron

Get depressed when: life is full of conflict, they have to face a personal confrontation, no one wants to help, the buck stops with them

Are afraid of: having to deal with a major personal problem, being left holding the bag, making major changes

Like people who: will make decisions for them, will recognize their strengths, will not ignore them, will give them respect

Dislike people who: are too pushy, too loud, and expect too much of them

Are valuable in work because they: mediate between contentious people, objectively solve problems

Could improve if they: set goals and became self-motivated, were willing to do more and move faster than expected, could face their own problems as well as they handle those of others

As leaders they: keep calm, cool, and collected, don't make impulsive decisions, don't often come up with brilliant new ideas

Reaction to stress: hide from it, watch TV, eat, tune out life

Recognized by their: calm approach, relaxed posture (sitting or leaning when possible)

209

PERSONALITY PROFILE

On the following pages you'll find a personality profile that will help you determine your personality. In each row of four words, place an X in front of the one word that most often applies to you. Continue through all forty lines. If you're not sure which word most applies to you, ask your spouse or a friend to help you. Use the word definitions following the test for the most accurate results.

Once you've completed the profile, transfer your answers to the scoring sheet. Add up your total number of responses in each column and combine your totals from the strengths and weaknesses sections. Then you'll be able to see your dominant personality type. You'll also see what combination of personalities you are. If, for example, your score is 35 in Powerful Choleric strengths and weaknesses, there's really little doubt. You're nearly all Powerful Choleric. But if your score is, for example, 16 in Powerful Choleric, 14 in Melancholy, and 5 in each of the others, you're a Powerful Choleric with a strong Perfect Melancholy.

Personality Profile

PLACE AN X IN FRONT OF THE ONE WORD
ON EACH LINE THAT MOST OFTEN APPLIES TO YOU.

Strengths

1 __ Adventurous	__ Adaptable	__ Animated	__ Analytical
2 __ Persistent	__ Playful	__ Persuasive	__ Peaceful
3 __ Submissive	__ Self-sacrificing	__ Sociable	__ Strong-willed
4 __ Considerate	__ Controlled	__ Competitive	__ Convincing
5 __ Refreshing	__ Respectful	__ Reserved	__ Resourceful
6 __ Satisfied	__ Sensitive	__ Self-reliant	__ Spirited
7 __ Planner	__ Patient	__ Positive	__ Promoter
8 __ Sure	__ Spontaneous	__ Scheduled	__ Shy
9 __ Orderly	__ Obliging	__ Outspoken	__ Optimistic
10 __ Friendly	__ Faithful	__ Funny	__ Forceful
11 __ Daring	__ Delightful	__ Diplomatic	__ Detailed
12 __ Cheerful	__ Consistent	__ Cultured	__ Confident
13 __ Idealistic	__ Independent	__ Inoffensive	__ Inspiring
14 __ Demonstrative	__ Decisive	__ Dry humor	__ Deep
15 __ Mediator	__ Musical	__ Mover	__ Mixes easily
16 __ Thoughtful	__ Tenacious	__ Talker	__ Tolerant
17 __ Listener	__ Loyal	__ Leader	__ Lively
18 __ Contented	__ Chief	__ Chart maker	__ Cute
19 __ Perfectionist	__ Pleasant	__ Productive	__ Popular
20 __ Bouncy	__ Bold	__ Behaved	__ Balanced

Weaknesses

21 __ Blank	__ Bashful	__ Brassy	__ Bossy
22 __ Undisciplined	__ Unsympathetic	__ Unenthusiastic	__ Unforgiving
23 __ Reticent	__ Resentful	__ Resistant	__ Repetitious
24 __ Fussy	__ Fearful	__ Forgetful	__ Frank
25 __ Impatient	__ Insecure	__ Indecisive	__ Interrupts
26 __ Unpopular	__ Uninvolved	__ Unpredictable	__ Unaffectionate
27 __ Headstrong	__ Haphazard	__ Hard to please	__ Hesitant
28 __ Plain	__ Pessimistic	__ Proud	__ Permissive
29 __ Angered easily	__ Aimless	__ Argumentative	__ Alienated

Appendix C

30 __ Naïve	__ Negative attitude	__ Nervy	__ Nonchalant
31 __ Worrier	__ Withdrawn	__ Workaholic	__ Wants credit
32 __ Too sensitive	__ Tactless	__ Timid	__ Talkative
33 __ Doubtful	__ Disorganized	__ Domineering	__ Depressed
34 __ Inconsistent	__ Introvert	__ Intolerant	__ Indifferent
35 __ Messy	__ Moody	__ Mumbles	__ Manipulative
36 __ Slow	__ Stubborn	__ Show-off	__ Skeptical
37 __ Loner	__ Lord over others	__ Lazy	__ Loud
38 __ Sluggish	__ Suspicious	__ Short-tempered	__ Scatterbrained
39 __ Revengeful	__ Restless	__ Reluctant	__ Rash
40 __ Compromising	__ Critical	__ Crafty	__ Changeable

Created by Fred Littauer

Scoring Sheet

<small>TRANSFER YOUR Xs FROM THE PREVIOUS PAGES TO THE APPROPRIATE COLUMNS BELOW.</small>

Strengths

	Popular Sanguine	Powerful Choleric	Perfect Melancholy	Peaceful Phlegmatic
1	__ Animated	__ Adventurous	__ Analytical	__ Adaptable
2	__ Playful	__ Persuasive	__ Persistent	__ Peaceful
3	__ Sociable	__ Strong-willed	__ Self-sacrificing	__ Submissive
4	__ Convincing	__ Competitive	__ Considerate	__ Controlled
5	__ Refreshing	__ Resourceful	__ Respectful	__ Reserved
6	__ Spirited	__ Self-reliant	__ Sensitive	__ Satisfied
7	__ Positive	__ Promoter	__ Planner	__ Patient
8	__ Spontaneous	__ Sure	__ Scheduled	__ Shy
9	__ Optimistic	__ Outspoken	__ Orderly	__ Obliging
10	__ Funny	__ Forceful	__ Faithful	__ Friendly
11	__ Delightful	__ Daring	__ Detailed	__ Diplomatic
12	__ Cheerful	__ Confident	__ Cultured	__ Consistent
13	__ Inspiring	__ Independent	__ Idealistic	__ Inoffensive
14	__ Demonstrative	__ Decisive	__ Deep	__ Dry humor
15	__ Mixes easily	__ Mover	__ Musical	__ Mediator
16	__ Talker	__ Tenacious	__ Thoughtful	__ Tolerant
17	__ Lively	__ Leader	__ Loyal	__ Listener
18	__ Cute	__ Chief	__ Chart maker	__ Contented
19	__ Popular	__ Productive	__ Perfectionist	__ Pleasant
20	__ Bouncy	__ Bold	__ Behaved	__ Balanced

TOTAL—STRENGTHS

_____   _____   _____   _____

213

Weaknesses

	Popular Sanguine	Powerful Choleric	Perfect Melancholy	Peaceful Phlegmatic
21	__ Brassy	__ Bossy	__ Bashful	__ Blank
22	__ Undisciplined	__ Unsympathetic	__ Unforgiving	__ Unenthusiastic
23	__ Repetitious	__ Resistant	__ Resentful	__ Reticent
24	__ Forgetful	__ Frank	__ Fussy	__ Fearful

25 __ Interrupts	__ Impatient	__ Insecure	__ Indecisive
26 __ Unpredictable	__ Unaffectionate	__ Unpopular	__ Uninvolved
27 __ Haphazard	__ Headstrong	__ Hard to please	__ Hesitant
28 __ Permissive	__ Proud	__ Pessimistic	__ Plain
29 __ Angered easily	__ Argumentative	__ Alienated	__ Aimless
30 __ Naïve	__ Nervy	__ Negative attitude	__ Nonchalant
31 __ Wants credit	__ Workaholic	__ Withdrawn	__ Worrier
32 __ Talkative	__ Tactless	__ Too sensitive	__ Timid
33 __ Disorganized	__ Domineering	__ Depressed	__ Doubtful
34 __ Inconsistent	__ Intolerant	__ Introvert	__ Indifferent
35 __ Messy	__ Manipulative	__ Moody	__ Mumbles
36 __ Show-off	__ Stubborn	__ Skeptical	__ Slow
37 __ Loud	__ Lord over others	__ Loner	__ Lazy
38 __ Scatterbrained	__ Short-tempered	__ Suspicious	__ Sluggish
39 __ Restless	__ Rash	__ Revengeful	__ Reluctant
40 __ Changeable	__ Crafty	__ Critical	__ Compromising

TOTAL—STRENGTHS

_____   _____   _____   _____

COMBINED TOTALS

_____   _____   _____   _____

Personality Test Word Definitions

STRENGTHS

———————1———————

Adventurous. Takes on new and daring enterprises with a determination to master them.

Adaptable. Easily fits and is comfortable in any situation.

Animated. Full of life; lively use of hand, arm, and facial gestures.

Analytical. Likes to examine the parts for their logical and proper relationships.

—— 2 ——

Persistent. Sees one project through to its completion before starting another.

Playful. Full of fun and good humor.

Persuasive. Convinces through logic and fact rather than charm or power.

Peaceful. Seems undisturbed and tranquil and retreats from any form of strife.

—— 3 ——

Submissive. Easily accepts any other's point of view or desire with little need to assert his own opinion.

Self-sacrificing. Willingly gives up her own personal needs for the sake of, or to meet the needs of, others.

Sociable. Sees being with others as an opportunity to be cute and entertaining rather than as a challenge or business opportunity.

Strong-willed. Determined to have his own way.

—— 4 ——

Considerate. Has regard for the needs and feelings of others.

Controlled. Has emotional feelings but rarely displays them.

Competitive. Turns every situation, happening, or game into a contest and always plays to win!

Convincing. Can win you over to anything through the sheer charm of her personality.

215

—— 5 ——

Refreshing. Renews and stimulates or makes others feel good.

Respectful. Treats others with deference, honor, and esteem.

Reserved. Self-restrained in expression of emotion or enthusiasm.

Resourceful. Able to act quickly and effectively in virtually all situations.

6

Satisfied. Easily accepts any circumstance or situation.

Sensitive. Intensively cares about others and about what happens.

Self-reliant. Can fully rely on his own capabilities, judgment, and resources.

Spirited. Full of life and excitement.

7

Planner. Prefers to work out a detailed arrangement beforehand for the accomplishment of a project or goal and prefers involvement with the planning stages and the finished product rather than the carrying out of the task.

Patient. Unmoved by delay, remains calm and tolerant.

Positive. Knows a situation will turn out right if she is in charge.

Promoter. Urges or compels others to go along, join, or invest through the charm of his personality.

8

Sure. Confident, rarely hesitates or wavers.

Spontaneous. Prefers all of life to be impulsive, unpremeditated activity, not restricted by plans.

Scheduled. Makes, and lives, according to a daily plan, dislikes her plan to be interrupted.

Shy. Quiet, doesn't easily initiate a conversation.

9

Orderly. Has a methodical, systematic arrangement of things.

Obliging. Accommodating, quick to do a task another's way.

Outspoken. Speaks frankly and without reserve.

Optimistic. Sunny disposition, convinces self and others that everything will turn out all right.

10

Friendly. Responds rather than initiates, seldom starts a conversation.

Faithful. Consistently reliable, steadfast, loyal, and devoted, sometimes beyond reason.

Funny. Sparkling sense of humor that can make virtually any story into a hilarious event.

Forceful. A commanding personality against whom others would hesitate to take a stand.

<hr />
11

Daring. Willing to take risks, fearless, bold.

Delightful. Upbeat and fun to be with.

Diplomatic. Deals with people tactfully, sensitively, and patiently.

Detailed. Does everything in proper order with a clear memory of all the things that happen.

<hr />
12

Cheerful. Consistently in good spirits and promoting happiness in others.

Consistent. Stays emotionally on an even keel, responding as one might expect.

Cultured. Interests involve both intellectual and artistic pursuits, such as theater, symphony, ballet.

Confident. Self-assured and certain of own ability and success.

<hr />
13

Idealistic. Visualizes things in their perfect form and has a need to measure up to that standard.

Independent. Self-sufficient, self-supporting, self-confident, and seems to have little need of help.

Inoffensive. Never says or causes anything unpleasant or objectionable.

Inspiring. Encourages others to work, join, or be involved, and makes the whole thing fun.

<hr />
14

Demonstrative. Openly expresses emotion, especially affection, and doesn't hesitate to touch others while speaking to them.

Decisive. Quick, conclusive, judgment-making ability.

Dry humor. Exhibits "dry wit," usually one-liners that can be sarcastic in nature.

Deep. Intense and often introspective with a distaste for surface conversation and pursuits.

-----15-----

Mediator. Consistently finds himself in the role of reconciling differences to avoid conflict.

Musical. Participates in or has a deep appreciation for music, is committed to music as an art form rather than for the fun of performance.

Mover. Driven by a need to be productive, is a leader whom others follow, finds it difficult to sit still.

Mixes easily. Loves a party and can't wait to meet everyone in the room, never meets a stranger.

-----16-----

Thoughtful. Considerate, remembers special occasions and is quick to make a kind gesture.

Tenacious. Holds on firmly, stubbornly, and won't let go until the goal is accomplished.

Talker. Constantly talking, generally telling funny stories and entertaining everyone around, feeling the need to fill the silence to make others comfortable.

Tolerant. Easily accepts the thoughts and ways of others without the need to disagree with or change them.

-----17-----

Listener. Always seems willing to hear what you have to say.

Loyal. Faithful to a person, ideal, or job, sometimes beyond reason.

Leader. A natural-born director who is driven to be in charge and often finds it difficult to believe that anyone else can do the job as well.

Lively. Full of life, vigorous, energetic.

-----18-----

Contented. Easily satisfied with what she has, rarely envious.

Chief. Commands leadership and expects people to follow.

Chart maker. Organizes life, tasks, and problem solving by making lists, forms, or graphs.

Cute. Precious, adorable, center of attention.

19

Perfectionist. Places high standards on self, and often on others, desiring that everything be in proper order at all times.

Pleasant. Easygoing, easy to be around, easy to talk with.

Productive. Must constantly be working or achieving, often finds it very difficult to rest.

Popular. Life of the party and therefore much desired as a party guest.

20

Bouncy. A bubbly, lively personality, full of energy.

Bold. Fearless, daring, forward, unafraid of risk.

Behaved. Consistently desires to conduct himself within the realm of what he feels is proper.

Balanced. Stable, middle-of-the-road personality, not subject to sharp highs or lows.

WEAKNESSES

21

Blank. Shows little facial expression or emotion.

Bashful. Shrinks from getting attention, resulting from self-consciousness.

Brassy. Showy, flashy, comes on strong, too loud.

Bossy. Commanding, domineering, sometimes overbearing in adult relationships.

22

Undisciplined. Lack of order permeates most every area of her life.

Unsympathetic. Finds it difficult to relate to the problems or hurts of others.

Unenthusiastic. Tends to not get excited, often feeling it won't work anyway.

Unforgiving. Has difficulty forgiving or forgetting a hurt or injustice done to him, apt to hold on to a grudge.

23

Reticent. Unwilling or struggles against getting involved, especially in complex situations.

Resentful. Often holds ill feelings as a result of real or imagined offenses.

Resistant. Strives, works against, or hesitates to accept any way other than her own.

Repetitious. Retells stories and incidents to entertain you without realizing he has already told the story several times before, is constantly needing something to say.

24

Fussy. Insistent over petty matters or details, calls for great attention to trivial details.

Fearful. Often experiences feelings of deep concern, apprehension, or anxiety.

Forgetful. Lack of memory, which is usually tied to a lack of discipline and not bothering to mentally record things that aren't fun.

Frank. Straightforward, outspoken, doesn't mind telling you exactly what she thinks.

25

Impatient. Finds it difficult to endure irritation or wait for others.

Insecure. Apprehensive or lacks confidence.

Indecisive. Finds it difficult to make any decision at all. (Not the personality that labors long over each decision to make the perfect one.)

Interrupts. More of a talker than a listener, starts speaking without even realizing someone else is already speaking.

26

Unpopular. Intensity and demand for perfection can push others away.

Uninvolved. Has no desire to listen or become interested in clubs, groups, activities, or other people's lives.

Unpredictable. May be ecstatic one moment and down the next, or willing to help but then disappears, or promises to come but forgets to show up.

Unaffectionate. Finds it difficult to verbally or physically demonstrate tenderness.

27

Headstrong. Insists on having his own way.

Haphazard. Has no consistent way of doing things.

Hard to please. Standards are set so high that it is difficult to ever satisfy her.

Hesitant. Slow to get moving and hard to get involved.

28

Plain. A middle-of-the-road personality without highs or lows and showing little, if any, emotion.

Pessimistic. While hoping for the best, generally sees the down side of a situation first.

Proud. Has great self-esteem and sees self as always right and the best person for the job.

Permissive. Allows others (including children) to do as they please to keep from being disliked.

29

Angered easily. Has a childlike flash-in-the-pan temper that expresses itself in tantrum style and is over and forgotten almost instantly.

Aimless. Not a goalsetter, with little desire to be one.

Argumentative. Incites arguments generally because he is right no matter what the situation may be.

Alienated. Easily feels estranged from others, often because of insecurity or fear that others don't really enjoy her company.

30

Naïve. Simple and childlike perspective, lacking sophistication or comprehension of what the deeper levels of life are really about.

Negative attitude. Attitude is seldom positive and is often able to see only the down or dark side of each situation.

Nervy. Full of confidence, fortitude, and sheer guts, often in a negative sense.

Nonchalant. Easygoing, unconcerned, indifferent.

31

Worrier. Consistently feels uncertain, troubled, or anxious.

Withdrawn. Pulls back and needs a great deal of alone or isolation time.

Workaholic. An aggressive goalsetter who must be constantly productive and feels very guilty when resting, is not driven by a need for perfection or completion but by a need for accomplishment and reward.

Wants credit. Thrives on the credit or approval of others; as an entertainer, this person feeds on the applause, laughter, and/or acceptance of an audience.

32

Too sensitive. Overly introspective and easily offended when misunderstood.

Tactless. Sometimes expresses himself in a somewhat offensive and inconsiderate way.

Timid. Shrinks from difficult situations.

Talkative. An entertaining, compulsive talker who finds it difficult to listen.

33

Doubtful. Characterized by uncertainty and lack of confidence that a problem situation will ever work out.

Disorganized. Lacks ability to get life in order.

Domineering. Compulsively takes control of situations and/or people, usually telling others what to do.

Depressed. Feels down much of the time.

34

Inconsistent. Erratic, contradictory, with actions and emotions not based on logic.

Introvert. Thoughts and interests are directed inward, lives within herself.

Intolerant. Appears unable to withstand or accept another's attitudes, point of view, or way of doing things.

Indifferent. Most things don't matter one way or the other.

_____35_____

Messy. Lives in a state of disorder, unable to find things.

Moody. Doesn't get very high emotionally, but easily slips into low lows, often when feeling unappreciated.

Mumbles. Will talk quietly under the breath when pushed, doesn't bother to speak clearly.

Manipulative. Influences or manages shrewdly or deviously for his own advantage, _will_ get his way somehow.

_____36_____

Slow. Doesn't often act or think quickly, too much of a bother.

Stubborn. Determined to exert their own will, not easily persuaded, obstinate.

Show-off. Needs to be the center of attention, wants to be watched.

Skeptical. Disbelieving, questioning the motive behind the words.

_____37_____

Loner. Requires a lot of private time and tends to avoid other people.

Lord over others. Doesn't hesitate to let you know that he is right and in control.

Lazy. Evaluates work or activity in terms of how much energy it will take.

Loud. Laugh or voice can be heard above others in the room.

_____38_____

Sluggish. Slow to get started, needs push to be motivated.

Suspicious. Tends to suspect or distrust others or their ideas.

Short-tempered. Has a demanding impatience-based anger and a short fuse, anger is expressed when others are not moving fast enough or have not completed what they have been asked to do.

Scatterbrained. Lacks the power of concentration or attention, flighty.

---39---

Revengeful. Knowingly or otherwise holds a grudge and punishes the offender, often by subtly withholding friendship or affection.

Restless. Likes constant new activity because it isn't fun to do the same things all the time.

Reluctant. Unwilling to or struggles against getting involved.

Rash. May act hastily, without thinking things through, generally because of impatience.

---40---

Compromising. Will often relax their position, even when right, in order to avoid conflict.

Critical. Constantly evaluating and making judgments, frequently thinking or expressing negative reactions.

Crafty. Shrewd, can always find a way to get to the desired end.

Changeable. Has a childlike, short attention span, needs a lot of change and variety to keep from getting bored.